FROM THE GROUND UP

The New City Books series explores the intersection of architecture, landscape architecture, infrastructure, and planning in the redevelopment of the civic realm. Focusing on government sponsorship of design, the study of weak-market cities, contemporary American housing, and the role of a research university as a resource and collaborator, the series highlights the formative nature of innovative design and the necessity for strategies that trigger public and private support.

The New City Books series includes:

From the Ground Up
Innovative Green Homes

Formerly Urban
Projecting Rust Belt Futures

New Public Works
Architecture, Planning, and Politics

Modern American Housing
High-Rise, Reuse, Infill

American City "X"
Syracuse after the Master Plan

FROM THE GROUND UP

INNOVATIVE GREEN HOMES

Edited by Peggy Tully

With essays by
Mark Robbins
Michael Sorkin
Susan Henderson

Photographs by
Richard Barnes

Syracuse University
School of Architecture
and
Princeton Architectural Press

Published by
Princeton Architectural Press
37 East Seventh Street
New York, New York 10003
Visit our website at www.papress.com.

Syracuse University School of Architecture
Slocum Hall
Syracuse, New York 13244
www.soa.syr.edu

© 2012 Princeton Architectural Press

Printed and bound in China

15 14 13 12 4 3 2 1 First edition

Series Editor: Mark Robbins

Design: Pentagram

Project Editor: Dan Simon

Special thanks to: Bree Anne Apperley,
Sara Bader, Janet Behning, Nicola Bednarek
Brower, Fannie Bushin, Megan Carey,
Carina Cha, Andrea Chlad, Russell Fernandez,
Will Foster, Jan Haux, Jennifer Lippert,
Gina Morrow, Katharine Myers, Margaret
Rogalski, Elana Schlenker, Sara Stemen,
Paul Wagner, and Joseph Weston of Princeton
Architectural Press—Kevin C. Lippert, publisher

The New City Books series is made possible
by a grant from the Rockefeller Foundation.
Additional funding is provided by the
Syracuse University School of Architecture,
Judith Greenberg Seinfeld, the National
Endowment for the Arts, The Richard H.
Driehaus Foundation, the Graham Foundation
for Advanced Studies in the Fine Arts, the New
York State Council for the Arts, Deutsche Bank
Americas Foundation, Furthermore: a program
of the J. M. Kaplan Fund, and the Central New
York Community Foundation.

Library of Congress
Cataloging-in-Publication Data

From the ground up: innovative green homes
/ edited by Peggy Tully; with essays by Mark
Robbins, Michael Sorkin, Susan Henderson—
First [edition].

pages cm — (New city books)

Includes bibliographical references.

ISBN 978-1-61689-092-6 (hardcover: alk.
paper)

1. Ecological houses. 2. Architecture,
Domestic—Environmental aspects. 3.
Sustainable architecture.
NA7117.5.F76 2012

728'.37047—dc23

2012002810

Contents

PREFACE

The From the Ground Up competition launched in the summer of 2008 with a call for submissions that asked entrants to imagine innovative and affordable single-family houses for infill sites in the Near Westside of Syracuse, New York. This neighborhood comprises 550 acres of industrial, residential, and commercial buildings adjacent to the city's center and, like many similar neighborhoods nationwide, has a pattern of vacant and condemned buildings among empty building lots. This familiar scenario belies a culturally vibrant place.

The goal of From the Ground Up was to spur thinking about potential models for such urban residential neighborhoods by creating new cost- and energy-efficient houses that are sensitive to the scale and composition of this ubiquitous American landscape. Seven selected teams made proposals for small single-family homes, three of which were ultimately built and sold to families who now live in the neighborhood.

The following pages present the design proposals of the seven finalists in the competition, along with photographs of the three houses that were built. Each of these demonstrates the contribution of attentive, progressive architecture and the value of advanced design and technology in developing sustainable prototypes. Our hope is that this modest project will be catalytic not only for the Near Westside but also for neighborhoods across the country.

ACKNOWL-EDGMENTS

The From the Ground Up design competition and resulting built houses were intensely collaborative projects. The level of innovation and the high expectations for design and construction involved in this project brought challenges that could not have been met without broad agreement among partners about the reasons to engage in such an undertaking. Kerry Quaglia, executive director of Home HeadQuarters, a private not-for-profit development company, was critical in this regard. His openness to expanding traditional models of providing housing offered a truly productive affiliation. Marilyn Higgins, vice president of community engagement and economic development at Syracuse University, oversees the Near Westside Initiative with eternal optimism, patience, and creativity, and her support was invaluable. Thanks as well to Edward Bogucz, executive director of the Syracuse Center of Excellence in Environmental and Energy Systems, for his interest in architecture and his insight and commitment to technology and sustainability. David C. Nutting, CEO and chairman of VIP Structures, a Syracuse-based design-build firm, contributed crucial expertise during the construction of the houses. The Central New York Community Foundation and the Community Preservation Corporation provided additional support for the competition. As with many of the university's innovative projects across disciplines, From the Ground Up was made possible within the environment supported by Chancellor Nancy Cantor's vision of scholarship in action.

Casey Jones provided welcome assistance to the School of Architecture in organizing and managing the competition. In addition to myself, Edward Bogucz, Marilyn Higgins, and Kerry Quaglia, the competition jury was composed of Barry Bergdoll, the Philip Johnson chief curator of architecture and design, the Museum of Modern Art; Julia Czerniak, director, UPSTATE: A Center for Design, Research, and Real Estate at the Syracuse University School of Architecture; Julie Eizenberg, principal, Koning Eizenberg Architecture; Bethaida Gonzalez, president, Syracuse Common Council; Carole Horan, Near Westside resident; David Lewis, principal, Lewis.Tsurumaki .Lewis; and Jason Pearson, president and CEO, GreenBlue.

This group engaged in a productive discussion during the selection process, bringing insight to an array of issues raised by housing and the single-family home, from the pragmatic to the stylistic and ideological. Their vision, rigor, and contributions to the ongoing debate were invaluable. I also thank Peter Larson, principal, Ashley McGraw Architects, and Sam Mason, Atelier Ten, consulting environmental designers, for their assistance in providing cost analysis and technical reports for each of the seven finalists for the use of the jury.

The depth of responses to the call for entries underscores the persistent interest among architects in this building type even in the still strong economy of early 2008. I thank all of those who submitted ideas and the finalists who produced schemes that could excite and provoke discussion among the jury and the community at large. The enthusiasm of the competition winners—Architecture Research Office/Della Valle Bernheimer, Cook+Fox Architects, and Onion Flats—reflected an unflagging commitment to the goals of the project from design through construction. Each team demonstrated a willingness to engage with all institutional partners to get the best work possible, and the homes that were built are a record of this collaborative process.

From the Ground Up was first presented at an exhibition I curated at Syracuse University School of Architecture's Slocum Gallery in January 2009 in parallel with a symposium with the winning architects and the competition organizers. The exhibition was designed and developed by the staff at UPSTATE: A Center for Design, Research, and Real Estate. Many thanks go to assistant director Joe Sisko and to UPSTATE: research fellow Jacob Brown, who coordinated the competition and exhibition and whose dedication and easy manner were a great asset to the project. Special thanks are due to the School of Architecture's Exhibition Committee, led by assistant professor Marissa Tirone and associate professor Jean François Bédard, and to the students who worked with them, including Timothy Gale, Stephen Klimek, Nilus Klingel, William Murillo, and Christina Webb.

I would also like to express thanks to Van Alen Institute, in particular the institute's chair of the board of trustees, Abby Hamlin, and then executive director Adi Shamir. They were instrumental in bringing the exhibition to New York City in May 2009 and hosting a public forum with the architects and project organizers led by Karrie Jacobs.

This book would not have been possible without the hard work of a committed band at the School of Architecture. Peggy Tully, UPSTATE: research fellow, brought this project to fruition with intelligence and aplomb. For their encouragement and support of the New City Books series, I would like to thank Julia Czerniak, assistant dean Katryn Hansen, and Mary Kate O'Brien, director of communications and media relations.

For their contributions to this book, I am extremely grateful to Susan Henderson and Michael Sorkin, whose essays offer valuable insights into the issues of affordable and sustainable housing in Syracuse and, more broadly, America's deindustrialized cities. I also would like to thank Richard Barnes, whose beautiful and intelligent photographs show the three From the Ground Up houses as they were sited and lived in, adding an extra dimension to the understanding of the way design works in the world.

At Princeton Architectural Press, I would like to thank Jennifer Lippert for her interest in and support of the issues explored in the series, and editors Megan Carey and Dan Simon for their careful and intelligent review of the final manuscript and images. The designers at Pentagram—Joe Marianek and Hamish Smyth, led by Michael Bierut— provided a cohesive look and feel for the series while incorporating a distinctive identity for each of the five books. Finally, I am thankful to Karen Stein for her intellect and counsel in the development of this book and the series as a whole, and to Kate Norment, who kept us all on track with a steady yet firm hand.

The New City Books series was made possible by a grant from the Rockefeller Foundation. Additional support was provided by the Syracuse University School of Architecture, Judith Greenberg Seinfeld, the National Endowment for the Arts, the Richard H. Driehaus Foundation, the Graham Foundation for Advanced Studies in the Fine Arts, the New York State Council for the Arts, Deutsche Bank Americas Foundation, Furthermore Grants in Publishing, and the Central New York Community Foundation.

This book is dedicated to the residents of the Near Westside and the members of the board of the Near Westside Initiative for their optimism, hard work, and collective vision.

Mark Robbins
Dean, Syracuse University School of Architecture

ARCHITEC-
TURE
OF THE
PRESENT
MARK
ROBBINS

A history of modern architecture can be read through the evolution
of the single-family home. Each generation has sought to improve upon
earlier iterations, rethinking and reinventing this seemingly simple
building type, projecting onto it a host of ideas about domestic life.
At certain historic moments, this has given form to radically different
configurations of the home and community. The current necessity for
sustainability provides urgency and a unique opportunity to take up the
problem again, designing affordable houses that respond to economic,
social, and environmental challenges.

The From the Ground Up competition seeks to provide another model
for disinvested urban residential neighborhoods found throughout
the United States through the creation of affordable green homes.
Developed for vacant infill sites on Syracuse's Near Westside, the
proposals that are displayed here offer an array of innovative designs
for energy-efficient prototypes. In so doing, they provide a new vision
for the neighborhood, one that uses sustainable planning and home
design as the catalyst for neighborhood revitalization.

The Near Westside is located just outside the downtown core and
comprises some two hundred wood-frame houses, as well as schools,
public housing, and largely vacant commercial and warehouse structures. A tightly spaced, polyglot array of Queen Anne, Italianate, cottage,
and bungalow houses and industrial buildings—all clad and reclad,
painted and changed in use and form over the past hundred years—the
neighborhood provides a microcosm of the building types and social
fabric of Syracuse and of many neighborhoods found across the
country. The vibrant community reflects both an old and a newer
profile of immigration; the neighborhood is now nearly equally populated by Latinos, African Americans, and European Americans. The
median age is in the mid-twenties, and the median household income of
$14,500 makes it one of the poorest census tracts in the United
States. The Near Westside also has one of the lowest rates of home-
ownership, just 16.7 percent, and a vacancy rate of 20 percent.
It exemplifies many near-in urban neighborhoods with a large number

of vacant buildings, underutilized neighborhood schools, swaths of open land, and streets without trees.

As with similar communities across the country, it has not experienced the scale of redevelopment that has recast neighborhoods in cities like Washington, DC, Atlanta, and Seattle over the past forty years. Retaining residents and attracting people to live in these walkable communities made up of older housing stock have driven new infill projects and renovation. But in the most challenged municipalities, demolition is often the default case, as it is both cheaper and more politically expedient. The cost of renovating neglected houses is often beyond what the market will bear, and the public rhetoric used in speaking about such houses ("crime house," "crack house") supports their clearance as a sign of ridding the neighborhood of pathology.

The Near Westside can be seen as a catalog of American strategies for rebuilding residential sites. Cross- and bar-shaped, midrise, brick public housing from the 1950s and 1960s sits on superblock site plans that replaced the existing street network, altering neighborhood circulation patterns. These large blocks are surrounded by older housing stock and the varied fragments of smaller-scale housing efforts by local and national nonprofit organizations and private landlords. These range from suburban ranch-style houses set back on enlarged fenced-in lots to disconnected segments of row houses, and this mix of building types has become a visible marker of neighborhoods receiving aid. The issue is not the difference in style but the way newer projects and policies reflect a misreading of the fabric of the neighborhood and its density, which relies on the number of houses on the block, the relationship between them, and their relationship to the street.

The lack of coordinated development between different agencies and smaller private developers occurs in the absence of public oversight, which could both increase housing units and enhance the overall quality of the neighborhood. The design of a place is coincident with its programming as well as economic development. Coordinated efforts spur revitalization, and an informed entity providing professional expertise is critical in overall planning. The cities that have done best in this regard have established performance guidelines rather than stylistic guidelines for buildings and their siting, parking, lighting, and landscape. Many have retained original elements of their neighborhoods and, together with new infill housing, have created a market draw. This

Typical mix of residential and industrial buildings in Syracuse's Near Westside neighborhood

Previous pages:
Examples of building stock in the Near Westside

attention to planning is often found in communities in which property values are high and everything from environmental quality to lot sizes and quality of design is reviewed.

To speak in this context of the need for developing neighborhoods with sufficient density, landscaping, trees, and a positive image may seem beside the point, a lofty goal when housing is critical. It is, however, an argument about identity and economics and the ways in which architecture supports a long-range development horizon. The forms of the buildings, tight streets, small lots, and walkability— the essential ease with which children can get to their local school, for example, or allows small-scale retail to be supported—are all attractive neighborhood assets that can be mined. The choice is not either good design or getting people well housed, and providing livable houses requires creativity on all fronts. It is a challenge of the market-place and the municipality, one that architects have assayed for the last century.

The James Geddes Rowhouses, public housing completed in 1955 by the Syracuse Housing Authority

From the Ground Up stands in a long line of research-based initiatives that are rhetorical, disciplinary, and technologically inventive—none of which lessens the fact that families have been housed and the neigh-borhood has been changed by the presence of these new homes. They are both symbolic and an actual boost to a neighborhood that has seen little built in recent history, with the exceptions of addi-tional social service facilities, and that creates a sense of a positive future. New residents and members of the local community have been attracted by the hipness and the difference of the resulting houses, and each of these has sold for above the prevailing market rate.

This publication catalogs the designs of the seven finalists in the From the Ground Up international competition. Fifty-two design teams submitted booklets of relevant work and qualifications for review, from which three teams were chosen to join four preselected teams to advance to the next stage of the competition. These seven teams traveled to Syracuse for an information session, with presentations by community members and other project stakeholders, oand a tour of the neighborhood and the selected sites, as well as meetings with potential homeowners. Teams received R&D support and had eight weeks to develop designs for a low-cost sustainable home that could be built for $150,000, including fees and site work. The Syracuse Center of Excellence provided additional funding for those aspects of the design that support the realization of sustainable features.

The seven finalists presented models and drawings to a jury composed of a mix of architects, community members, an elected official, professors, and a curator of architecture. The three selected teams—Architecture Research Office/Della Valle Bernheimer, Cook+Fox Architects, and Onion Flats—were commissioned to develop their winning designs, and over the next year and a half they worked with the project sponsors to complete the houses, from construction documents through supervision of construction. The three houses now sit among the older homes (some on lots of original size) and feature the type of varied massing and surface found throughout the Near Westside.

The lineage of the project is also distinctly American in its focus on the single-family house, itself not an unproblematic assumption today. At the scale of three or even ten houses per year, this model doesn't approach the slim number of units produced in the few progressive American planned communities of the New Deal or the concerted national efforts of European housing demonstrations of the teens and twenties, with which it shared aspirations. The modest scale of our project belies the level of intellectual, administrative, and financial resources required to get these individual houses built. But the challenges one might have expected with prototypes were met with equal amounts of energy and good will. Together with the new institutional projects in the Near Westside, they will have an impact in a neighborhood of this size. The mix of uses, such as a headquarters for the public broadcasting station, live-work lofts, offices, and educational and cultural organizations, also recalls the complex programming of those earlier housing precedents, which more closely approximated urban density and richness. The houses push the limits of technology and form and, like their antecedents, provide built evidence for private and municipal financing that alternative approaches work.

The From the Ground Up competition was organized by the School of Architecture partnering with the Near Westside Initiative, the Center of Excellence, and Home HeadQuarters, a private not-for-profit housing agency. It was intended to create models for high-performance homes and to encourage a reconsideration of the city's approach to density and zoning. The existing social service models and city zoning policies have encouraged demolishing vacant houses, creating larger lot sizes, and fusing multiple lots into single-home sites with asphalt parking pads rather than on-street parking. Landlords and home-owners are encouraged to acquire adjacent lots for use as side yards,

At the groundbreaking ceremony for From the Ground Up (left to right):
Marilyn Higgins, vice president for community engagement and economic development, Syracuse University; Alys Mann, neighborhood planning and GIS manager, Home HeadQuarters; Kerry Quaglia, exectuve director, Home HeadQuarters; Edward Bogucz, executive director, Syracuse Center of Excellence in Environmental and Energy Systems; Carole Horan, Near Westside resident; Nancy Cantor, chancellor, Syracuse University; Mark Robbins, dean, Syracuse University School of Architecture; Jared Della Valle, principal, Della Valle Bernheimer; Rick Cook, principal, Cook+Fox Architects; Pam Campbell, senior associate, Cook+Fox Architects; Adam Yarinsky, principal, Architecture Research Office

further reducing the number of dwellings per block. The character and density of the walkable neighborhood of 33-by-100-foot lots have eroded in favor of a suburban model.

From the Ground Up exhibition, Slocum Gallery, Syracuse University School of Architecture, 2009

As a footnote, these houses will create a nucleus in the neighborhood for the work of several design studios dedicated to renovating houses, more in the manner of Gordon Matta-Clark perhaps than Laura Ashley. Students working with architect Frederick Stelle and professor Timothy Stenson have worked within the preexisting shell and wooden framework of the old houses, learning about their design potential as well as budgetary constraints. The intention is not to have students physically build the houses but to perform in a way that mirrors practice, providing the design, construction documents, and supervision in partnership with Home HeadQuarters and vip Structures. The first set of homes is under construction as of this writing, as the next round is being designed.

The proposals and the resulting houses featured in this book demonstrate the value of design within a typically underserved community and revisit the heroic modernist aspiration to bring architecture into the foreground in the discussion of housing and planning. The architects were ambitious in the forms of the houses they designed and their use of technology. It is hoped that this project will be catalytic in our neighborhoods, built on innovation, from the ground up.

W FAYETTE

MARCELLUS

SENECA

ONTARIO

BETH

OSWEGO

S GEDDES

GIFFORD

THE RESIL-IENT COMMU-NITY

SUSAN HENDERSON

Imagine ourselves as architects, all armed with a wide range of capacities and powers, embedded in a physical and social world full of manifest constraints and limitations. Imagine also that we are striving to change that world. As crafty architects bent on insurgency we have to think strategically and tactically about what to change and where, about how to change and what and with what tools. But we also have somehow to continue to live in this world. This is the fundamental dilemma that faces everyone interested in progressive change.

—David Harvey, *Spaces of Hope*[1]

The Near Westside in Syracuse is an unremarkable neighborhood, a commonplace in the Rust Belt terrain of Upstate New York. It is bounded on the north by rail lines and the path of the old Erie Canal; by a six-lane arterial on the east; by a busy arterial to the west, which crosses it without a passing glance; and by a neighborhood street on the south that is hardly a boundary at all, but simply a mark made to a planner's convenience (fig. 1). "Near West" refers to a proximity to the heart of the historic downtown district known as Armory Square, which lies just across the rail line to the east. Yet within its 194 acres lies a microcosm of the nineteenth-century city, battered but recognizable—a representative fragment. Remnants of industry, churches of various denominations, parks, and streets of modest, detached single-family houses characterize a parochial world. It is a community shaped by working-class life and varied ethnicities and religions, during an age when Syracuse was a vital industrial center. The neighborhood also had its distinguished buildings—in particular, the Catholic parish church of Saint Lucy's, designed by Archimedes Russell in 1873, and an industrial building for the H. H. Franklin Manufacturing Company, the first poured concrete structure in the city, designed by Albert Kahn in 1909.

On a spring day, the Near Westside is a lively place, with much sociability in evidence—children playing in the schoolyards and playgrounds and bicycling through the streets, neighbors talking,

Previous pages:
Fig. 1. Aerial view of Syracuse's Near Westside neighborhood showing location of From the Ground Up houses

Fig. 2. Detail of 1902 map of
Syracuse, with the Near Westside
neighborhood highlighted

and families gathered around the porches. This is a gift of the density of working-class, single-family houses with deep front porches set close to the street—a standard nineteenth-century type that populated the industrial neighborhoods of New York State and was built by developers or industrialists in cities like Syracuse, where land was relatively cheap and plentiful. One of the earliest such enclaves in town, the Near Westside was soon circled by industry on three sides, businesses that sprouted up in response to the rail and canal line that passed to the north (fig. 2). From the neighborhood, it was but a short walk to the factory or a short trolley ride into the center city. The needs of everyday life could be supplied by a trip to the neighborhood stores.

In the industrial economy, production for consumption was the driving force of the labors of the communities: Syracuse had eighty cigar factories and grew its own tobacco in the immediate area. Everything from canned goods—None Such Mincemeat was introduced by a local canning company—to plumbing and harnesses was made within walking distance of the Near Westside. Notable companies in the neighborhood included the Syracuse Chilled Plow Company, the major hand tool manufacturer Whitman and Barnes Manufacturing Company, and Case Supply. There were the railyards of the Delaware, Lackawanna, and Western line and turntable and repair services. Among this remarkable array was the "Syracuse Cradle of Industry," the C. E. Lipe Machine Shop on Geddes Street. In a small inauspicious block, Charles Lipe opened a gear manufactory in 1880. He was a prolific inventor—he invented a cigar-rolling machine, a two-speed gear for bicycles, a broom-winding machine, and more—and his shop became a center for industrial problem solving, a kind of local think tank. Henry Ford came here to oversee the construction of parts for his first Model T. And it was here that Herbert H. Franklin, owner of the world's first metal die-casting, small gear, and bearing manufactory, met John Wilkinson, designer of an air-cooled automobile. Their collaboration led to the formation of the Franklin Motor Company in 1902. After four years, the company ranked third among American automakers. By the mid-1920s, it was the largest company in the city, employing over 3,500 workers. Among its many buildings was the factory at 719 West Marcellus Street designed by Kahn. The Franklin Motor Company began a slow gathering of capital, transforming a company-based economy to a corporate one—a concentration that hastened as Franklin was absorbed by General Motors.

The transfer of the neighborhood from the working class to the poor who live here today followed on the postwar growth of the city's suburbs and the construction of highways through the downtown—that common chapter in the life of the American city. The second chapter, in the form of urban renewal, arrived in 1964 as Syracuse readied itself for a future that would never come, sweeping away large swaths of the industrial- and business-district fabric that would remain vacant for decades. In the Near Westside, this double blow came in a milder form. Highway ramps turned the neighborhood's western boundary into a barrier, and the insertion of two public-housing projects under the General Neighborhood Renewal Plan removed five blocks of single-family houses and two street segments, both disturbing the scale of the neighborhood fabric. On the other hand, the neighborhood was spared the more sweeping depredations of "slum clearance," retaining much of its original street pattern, infrastructure, and housing stock. Its factory buildings, now empty, remained.

Syracuse public housing from the urban renewal years is typical and largely unexceptional. There were two rather beautiful and innovative projects—both demolished in recent years—that evoked the idealism of the Great Society and the architect's aspirations to achieve something better for society's poor (fig. 3). More common were brick-clad slabs and towers set on large lawns. The Near Westside had four cross-axial towers. In these the relationship between work, community life, and dwelling was critically severed. Any capital development that might foster jobs would happen elsewhere; the housing, meanwhile, provided affordable rents in decent buildings, but in this severed landscape, the tenants had few communal or personal resources to redress their poverty, even on an ad hoc basis. The housing became little more than barracks.

Fig. 3. Abandoned Kennedy Square Housing development, Syracuse, New York; completed c. 1975, closed 2008

Today the Near Westside appears rather more interesting. With a population of 2,200, it is one of the poorest neighborhoods in the country. Half of its residents live below the poverty line, and some 37 percent are disabled. It has more than its share of crime. But unlike postwar suburbs and projects of the 1960s, it maintains a healthy infrastructure of services, and everyday needs are still met within its boundaries. It has the city's only remaining privately owned supermarket, and there are a smattering of other shops, bars, several churches, and a health clinic. A short walk under the underpass leads to Armory Square, and a small mall occupies an old industrial ground. There are also a good number of large and small green spaces, ballparks, and fields. And because the neighborhood is poor, car ownership is low and the streets are relatively free from traffic. The parish church of Saint Lucy's remains a stronghold of community engagement, and there are two major public schools within its boundaries. Indeed, but for its poverty, the Near Westside represents something of the golden age of the American neighborhood, a life that has been celebrated and a loss mourned by people from Jane Jacobs to Marshall Berman.

A reservoir of sorts lies in neighborhoods like the Near Westside. Absent state authorities, they have been left to abandonment and neglect. Yet there remains a preserve of housing and building stock, buildable lots, and communities with a base of social activism. It is safeguarded against gentrification by the lack of demand—by the sheer amount of housing stock available to a declining population. There is potential for a resilient community. This is what Syracuse University and Chancellor Nancy Cantor saw in 2005. Cantor, in consultation with Mark Robbins, dean of the school of architecture; Marilyn Higgins, president of economic development of National Grid (the regional electric company); and others, was seeking a project that could aid the city through a combination of funding and applied research performed by the university's store of talent. The university would invest $13.8 million, a sum equal to a loan payment it owed to the state; the debt was forgiven on the stipulation that the same amount would be applied to a project that was beneficial to the city of Syracuse. Its participation in the Near Westside Initiative (NWSI) was the result. A consortium of private and public agencies and neighborhood residents joined to form a nonprofit with additional moneys from private contributors and a Restore New York grant. The NWSI became one of several programs—including the Paducah Renaissance Alliance, the West Philadelphia Initiative, Minneapolis's Artspace USA, and the Over-the-Rhine community in Cincinnati—that were inspired by cultural reservoirs. Like them, the NWSI represents a coalition of institutions working together, but each also making its own contribution.

In practice the initiative is multivalent and opportunistic, engaging a variety of agencies, institutions, and grassroots organizers in a loose coalition. Robbins invokes the "third way" in describing the strategy. Historically rooted in progressive reform, the third way describes politically centrist and reconciliatory efforts—among private charities, network organizations, academics, and intellectuals—devoted to economic (i.e., distributive) democracy and to education and technology as paths to improvement. A similar idealism paired with pragmatism can be read in the NWSI. Today's reformers operate under very different conditions from their forebears. Rather than the rise of an immigrant working class, they contemplate the long wake of its collapse, with no remedy, no source of future prosperity for America's underclass in sight. And today's third way must rely on the modest momentum, as represented by the NWSI, in localized communities and singular efforts, rather than sweeping initiatives.

At the time that the university was forging an alliance with the NWSI, it was also expanding its presence in downtown. Due to the major thrust of Cantor's chancellorship and the program Scholarship in Action, which partners members of the university community with various constituents of the private and public sectors to address pressing public policy issues in the city of Syracuse, the university became active in the life and fortunes of the city. In 2005, during renovations on campus, the Syracuse University School of Architecture moved into a warehouse, which after purchase and remodel became the "Warehouse" and the first university building located downtown. Gluckman Mayner Architects renovated the building in the style of contemporary repurposing for which the firm had become known. Robbins saw the Warehouse as an anchor for the "cultural reweaving" of downtown institutions, a goal furthered by the Connective Corridor project, also begun in 2005. Here, the university, in collaboration with the city and National Grid, created a cultural and transit corridor to renew ties between University Hill and downtown and to reunite two entities sundered by slum clearance and the construction of the interstate highway. In 2007 the university and Centro, the municipal bus service, introduced a free Connective Corridor bus service between the campus and downtown. Other programs to enhance the streets along the corridor and to strengthen the pedestrian areas within the cultural and civic buildings of the downtown are ongoing. In 2010 the university built a new building in downtown on the city side of the corridor. Designed by Toshiko Mori, the Syracuse Center of Excellence sits a few blocks from the Warehouse. A LEED Platinum building, it is devoted to technological innovation in the areas of sustainability and environmental quality.

Cantor and Higgins, who had been appointed vice president of community engagement and economic development at Syracuse University, sought to make a particular contribution: to link the cultural project of the Connective Corridor with an emerging art community in the

industrial buildings that bordered the Near Westside. Situated at its
northern corner, the Delavan Art Gallery was converted to artists'
studios in the 1990s. Its success suggested that an artist-relocation
project might incentivize modest growth in the industrial borderland
while enhancing the community's cultural life. Purchasing the Lincoln
Warehouse, the university created thirteen live/work market apart-
ments and two floors of commercial space. The ground floor was
leased to La Casita Cultural Center Project, a child-education initiative
focusing on culture and the arts and sponsored by the nonprofit agency
Say Yes to Education. La Casita formed in 2008 with support from
Syracuse University, the Syracuse City School District, and the Latino
community. Another university purchase, an assembly of Case Supply
buildings adjacent to the Delavan Art Gallery, is undergoing conversion
to provide a new home for the city's public television and radio station
as well as an adult literacy center. The work is being done by the city's
venerable architecture firm King + King, which itself recently relo-
cated from the suburbs into a new LEED building positioned between
the Warehouse and the Near Westside.

Meanwhile, the School of Architecture pursued its own multifaceted
strategy, encompassing research, public dialogue, and pedagogy.
Robbins created UPSTATE: A Center for Design, Research, and
Real Estate as a platform for research, events, and symposia, in
order to build a dialogue among journalists, architects, and city offi-
cials. Located in the Warehouse, the center has pursued speculative
projects and was much involved with the Connective Corridor and
the NWSI. Through UPSTATE: Robbins focused on preserving the
grain and scale of the residential terrain of the Near Westside and its
modest single-family homes. He saw the greatest danger to the neighborhood's fabric in dated zoning policies that favored de-densification,
tear-downs, and suburban models of housing. At present, a variance
is required to make the neighborhood denser (i.e., more sustainable).
In wealthier neighborhoods, the historical character of both the
houses and the neighborhoods is jealously guarded as part of the real
and cultural capital of the homeowner. In poor neighborhoods like the
Near Westside, character is neglected in favor of prosaic amenities
that destroy the social and visual integrity of the street, such as deep
setbacks to provide parking in front of the house. The original lots
were narrow but deep, allowing for the keeping of horses and car-
riages. Contemporary zoning policy encourages larger lots with side
yards. Habitat for Humanity currently replaces each two-story house
with a one-story suburban model on a double lot set back from the

Fig. 4. Habitat for Humanity
house typology; this example
completed 2009

street (fig. 4). Suburbanizing practices weaken the neighborhood not only by decreasing the vibrancy of the street image and its architecture, but also by discouraging the sociability that the neighborhood exhibits so well. UPSTATE: research fellows produced a critique of these zoning practices for the Near Westside, and other studies demonstrated how overlay zoning would benefit the neighborhood by encouraging, for example, innovative uses of the open space and re-densification.

The second component of this research—the reconsideration of the single-family house—engendered the Near Westside competition, From the Ground Up: Innovative Green Homes, cosponsored by Syracuse University School of Architecture, Syracuse Center of Excellence, and Home HeadQuarters. One goal of the competition was to produce a more complex reading of the fabric and to make a case for maintaining it. Another goal was to apply innovative design thinking to low-cost housing in order to produce workable models that could be replicated here and elsewhere at a reasonable cost. New home construction and renovations have been ongoing in the Near Westside since 2008 by Habitat for Humanity and the nonprofit Christopher Community. The most active agency in the neighborhood is Home HeadQuarters, one of the largest nonprofit providers of affordable home and energy improvement to the underserved in New York State. In 2009 Home HeadQuarters purchased seventy-four houses and a number of vacant lots in the neighborhood. The organization renovates and then sells properties, builds new homes, and operates a homesteading program that sells selected houses for a dollar, under a guarantee of quick and sound renovation and owner occupancy for three years. Two Home HeadQuarters homestead houses in the Near Westside have been renovated by local artists. While these endeavors have great social value, the design value is not always equally compelling. The From the Ground Up competition exemplified research and innovation in the service of good design and planning practices. First, the competition brief reframed neighborhood revitalization in terms of sustainability, in the social and economic as well as environmental sense. The research dovetailed with the UPSTATE: study of neighborhood-wide sustainability, and together the two outlined a suggested blueprint for reconstruction.

The competition also addressed the wider professional community concerned with the prototypical conditions and issues represented by the Near Westside. The reconsideration of the modest single-family house by innovative architects in service to an underserved and diverse community may serve as a catalyst for improving neighborhoods elsewhere. The three competition houses each cost about double their selling price; the university subsidized the difference, a luxury that provided not only the opportunity to pursue innovation, but also an amenity to the neighborhood. This is not an economic solution, which leads to the question: how can funding for poor neighborhoods be sustained without public funding and beyond a windfall, in this instance provided by the university? Efforts to secure the NWSI are ongoing and are looking to corporate funding as a future source for the crafting of sustainable financing for coalition efforts. Robbins's hope is that such a coalition extends the scope of the program beyond the three houses represented by From the Ground Up. For a modestly sized neighborhood like the Near Westside, this is an approachable goal.

The questions raised by the From the Ground Up competition and the NWSI address fundamental issues of praxis beyond the designs themselves, much like those outlined by David Harvey in the epigraph, which was written concerning his own neighborhood of East Baltimore, Maryland. How does a professional, a university, or a community make a better city; what is the project; and more especially, what is the strategy? In our current situation, when the need is great but the coffers are largely empty, urban renewal policies of the 1960s hover like a Janus-faced parent. Blessed with tax funds and aspiring to shining modern cities, its policies exemplify the German concept of *Grossstadtfeindschaft*—a dread of the metropolis and particularly of the urban poor. We have nostalgia for an era when President Johnson's Great Society and War on Poverty recognized and sought to assuage the plight of the underprivileged, but we are stunned by the gashes of the interstate-highway system and the muddle of its housing projects. Whatever adjustments might have been made to social and design policy are out of reach, casualties of these infrastructural failures, damage compounded by Reagan-era privatization and supply-side economics. With regulatory controls on development and construction weakened, cultural and residential enclaves of the 1980s and 1990s reflected a deadening monoculture as social qualities, events, and solidarities were further eroded. The New Urbanism permeated the form but not the resident population of the nineteenth-century cities— for example, New York's, as Times Square was sanitized and a bland monoculture erased character and vitality from the city. In the long wave of American retreat from state programs on behalf of the poor, revitalization reemerges as a broad category of modest efforts aimed to reestablish the integrity of this communal morphology. It has proven its value. UPSTATE: argues for preserving what fragments of the neighborhood remain and, with them, what components of the community's sense of identity. Rather than demolition—a quick and easy sign of "improvement"—there is the potential to make something that lasts.

The From the Ground Up houses take neighborhood revitalization beyond the fix-up, setting novel forms in the streets of the Near Westside. In their peculiarity, they draw camera-wielding outsiders into a forgotten neighborhood; through the obvious investment of creativity and energy they represent, they inspire us. The potential for the community to be influenced by thoughtful interpretations of historical infrastructure is suggested by the reaction to a recent decision to tear down the nineteenth-century Blodgett Elementary School in the center of the Near Westside. An outcry among both the community and the initiative coalition reversed the decision, and the school is now slated for renovation. The From the Ground Up houses make us aware of social change in a unique way. Conditions have undergone a sea change since the industrial heyday when the neighborhood was first built. In the 1900s, the workplace was intimately tied to the neighborhood, surrounding it on every side. Today Near Westside pioneers are moving back to a kind of localized economy that approaches America in its preindustrial age of the eighteenth century. Entrepreneurs and adventurous spirits, artists, and inventors use their homes or cheap loft spaces to pioneer anew. The residents of the three From the Ground Up houses include artists and entrepreneurs, and the houses, in reflecting this shift in the economy, the nature of family, and the rest, embody this new life. For students, From the Ground Up serves as precedent-setting work directly related to their endeavors. Fourth-year design studios, taught by visiting critics like Brad Lynch and Julie Eizenberg, have researched innovative ways to reuse existing Near Westside building stock, addressing complex questions of environmental and economic sustainability and the nature of the contemporary family. In partnership with Home HeadQuarters, the School of Architecture is renovating derelict houses to studio designs, and students are hired to work on the construction documents during the summer months. One house, completed in 2009 and designed as part of a studio led by Lubrano Ciavarra, was constructed and sold. With an echo of the old Lipe shop, the Near Westside has evolved as a laboratory and a fieldwork site that offers a social microcosm small enough that the work will have a demonstrable impact.

Questions investigated in the Near Westside and the From the Ground Up competitions are: How can designers improve living conditions without a massive injection of public moneys? How can the profession help current residents achieve a better material existence without an a priori expectation of better jobs, higher incomes, and more tax revenue for infrastructure? The answer is at work here: on a modest scale but on many fronts and engaging many parties. Today's NWSI is an incomplete, multifaceted project, the terms and goals of which are in a constant state of negotiation and change. It is an endeavor resulting from an imperfect world, the collapse of the public sphere, and the reinvention of private charities and small public-private partnerships. The NWSI has made inroads on a variety of fronts, and its impact may be felt as an improvement in the lives of its residents and in the economy of the neighborhood. From the Ground Up shines new light on the issue of this overlooked type, the working-class single-family home, and through invention and reconfiguration furthers its restoration in a form reflecting contemporary life.

1   David Harvey, *Spaces of Hope* (Berkeley: University of California Press, 2000), 233.

THE STATE OF THE HOUSE

MICHAEL SORKIN

Can Architecture Save Us?

Syracuse is a deindustrialized and shrinking Rust Belt city. Its stock of homes is frayed and abandoned, its cityscape gapped, its project of manufacture failed, and its economy parlous. The city is a smaller version of Detroit, with its eviscerated core, or New Orleans, where long-festering animosity against the poor and the sudden production of new codes for speaking racism have left the city much smaller and whiter and where rebuilding efforts are focused on the neutralities of infrastructure and directed at those with the means to secure financial, political, and professional advantage. As with these two poster cities for American urban decline, the residue of natural and economic disaster paradoxically raises hope in the crying potential of their surplus voids. For architects, to hope is to build: our optimism can't stand the evil triage of the shrinking city.

New Orleans is the site of the recent development that most closely resembles From the Ground Up, actor Brad Pitt's Make It Right project. Architecture has been the front man, in both senses, making its mark in the right place—the Lower Ninth Ward—and the right people—displaced African American inhabitants. Make It Right, a totally well-meaning financial subvention, enabled famous architects to participate and houses to be built that were more substantial and more considered than a generic default. Other cultural agendas could also be served by the project, in particular a coup in the style wars against the neo-traditionalist tendency—widely embraced by local establishments—that was (fairly uselessly) perceived as an enemy camp. Syracuse also works to assert the relevance of contemporary architecture to contemporary problems (fig. 1).

These efforts are modest: a couple of dozen houses in the Lower Ninth, a few houses in the Near Westside. While it is great to make any authentic contribution to the housing question, these projects aspire to an influence beyond their numbers, and beyond Oprah-esque voluntarism—"You've got a house!" "You've got a house!" "You've got a house!" Amended: "You've got a *special* house!" A house that has

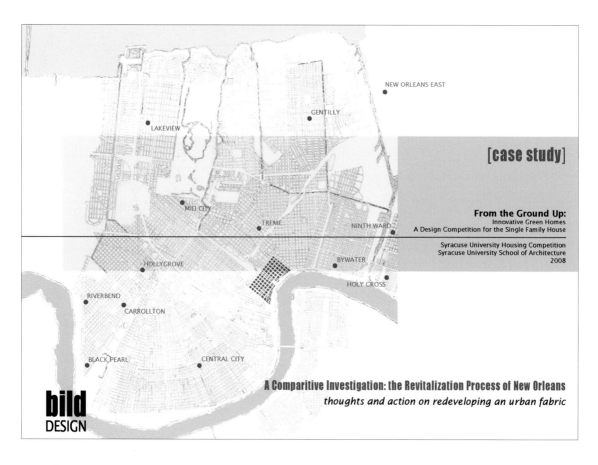

Fig. 1. Bild Design's proposal invoking
New Orleans as a precedent

Fig. 2. Konyk Architecture's
Hybrid House

been designed to protect itself from floods and that is deeply sensitive to environmental concerns. A house that is from the beautiful new.
But the small numbers beg the question of how visionary projects can
incite a far wider enthusiasm for building wisely and well.

The "model home" strategy begins from a singularity—the idea of the
"architect-designed" house, a house that is unlike those in its literal and
conceptual contexts. In New Orleans, this seems to be a point of pride
for dwellers, if sometimes a point of derision for observers. Of course,
Katrina swept the plate clean, and there's the powerful reality of that
context of no context but memory. The Make It Right houses stand as a
brave little *Siedlung*, pointing to a future in which our now-valued ideas
about the indispensability of difference demand we build an ark of the
nonconventional. The jury is surely still out on the precise relationship
of community and cacophony and the limits of a curatorial approach
to urbanism. But the effort is brave. The question remains, though,
of the media through which it's possible to look through the architect's

From the Ground Up: Innovative Green Homes
A Design Competition for the Single Family House

Presented by

Home HeadQuarters, Inc.   Syracuse Center of Excellence in   **SYRACUSE**
                                 Environmental and Energy Systems   **ARCHITECTURE**
                                                                          Syracuse University
                                                                          School of Architecture

A project of UPSTATE: A Center for Design, Research, and Real Estate at Syracuse University School of Architecture

For more information, go to soa.syr.edu/competition

Fig. 3. Poster announcing
From the Ground Up competition

signature to what can be generalized about best building practices for the demanding myriad of comparable sites and less flamboyant talents.

These singular houses certainly ask something about subjectivity: who are they for? The model homes of modernity were about minimalism, reproducibility, uniformity of subject and shelter, and an "industrial" style. Modernist planning practice was in thrall of the diagrammatic, yielding a certain quantitative style premised on fixed forms and relations, an end state, a utopia. The new houses in New Orleans and Syracuse are surely more astringent in their insistence that these structures be individuals, not clones. As models for a way of building at a time of changing consciousness about such critical matters as the relationship of architecture and the environment, of living and working, of the fate of the family, the variety is bracing. But architectural singularity does beg the question of the nature of its relationship to a public that is at once plural *and* full of critical affinities.

However the question of the singular is parsed, it's clear that the judgment of numbers is relevant. The environment is a constant, and its forces can be quantified according to laws that are fixed and calculable. Are these houses capable of withstanding the forces of water and wind? Do they consume lower amounts of energy? Are they constructed of sustainable materials? Will they reduce carbon loads? These are the quanta of quality by which all architecture must be judged and by which virtually all architecture falls short. Additionally, each of these houses attempts to respond to the beleaguering means test that often arrests sustainable construction: the work is economical and the strictures of common sense seem to crimp creativity not at all. By this standard these projects are a big success.

But with such success comes otherness. In many of the images prepared by contestants, the new designs are Photoshopped into views of the site on which they're to be built (fig. 2). Their context signifies the indigenous—clapboarded Carpenter Gothic homes that seem to be the neighborhood genus. Are the new houses good neighbors? In some global sense, of course they are. There's surely an expanded compass of neighborliness beyond keeping the yard neat and kids quiet that embraces the character of kindness visited on the planet via activists' greenness. The translation to form, though, raises many questions, and one might ask about the semiotics and the practicalities of arguing via a fresh visual paradigm versus a considered retrofit and revision of the familiar. Where to invest the signifying energy?

Both New Orleans and Syracuse make a clear and convinced investment in the singular. I was struck by the poster that advertised this competition, which presents a series of silhouettes of homely objects intended to signify a repertoire of domesticity (fig. 3). To me, the poster resembles one of those intelligence tests in which one is meant to identify the "inappropriate" object in the field. I got the pair of pliers, the potted plant, the rake, the swing set, the picnic table, but was not entirely sure what to make of the pineapple. It seemed like something out of the eighteenth century, a Georgian ornament, the newel post of the exotic, a symbol of colonial engorgement. What did it mean? Globalization? Food miles? Healthy dessert?

I think, though, that the pineapple is the right metaphor, an alien fruit planted in the field of the familiar. Going through the first phase of the project's fifty-odd submissions was a stimulating probe of a *new* familiar, of the discursive state of play of the profession, a survey that permitted a classification of tropes both sturdy and fresh that structured responses to a challenging brief. What grows in this plantation? Some hope.

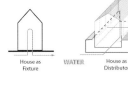

UTILITY DEPENDENCIES

House as air flow producer — **AIR** — House as air flow facilitator

Roof as energy / light container — **SKY** — Roof as energy / light provider

Ground as Foundation — **EARTH** — Ground as Buffer

House as Fixture — **WATER** — House as Distributor

TOPOLOGICAL OPPORTUNITIES

Fig. 4. Studio SUMO's diagram of energy usage

Passive Acceptance

The logic of sustainability begins with ventilation, orientation, and insolation. That this is the basis for virtually every project submitted is heartening. Even the more technologized solutions (mainly having to do with producing electrical energy) resist cutting-edge arcana in favor of the off-the-shelf (fig. 4). That this is not trumpeted but simply given suggests that architectural culture—at least at its creative end—has undergone a mighty, useful shift.

De Minimis

The received wisdom of "less is more" gets the treatment it deserves. Here the strategy is not argued visually, but economically and envi-ronmentally. A shortened perimeter and compact design add thermal efficiency. Less material costs less, uses less. The profit in this way of thinking is always at the margin—the point at which efficiency becomes discriminatory, punitive, the marker of a subject supposed to fail. Modernism has been circling this block for yonks, and, to be fair, most of the projects submitted go for elegance, not discipline. And elegance, the motto of all right-thinking engineers, is something to go for.

Community Values

An anxiety stalks the submissions, marked succinctly by one propos-ing "design cannot solve this problem" (fig. 5). This slogan marks the conceptual turbulence that makes doing a project like this so useful. But just what *is* the problem that cannot be solved by an inexpensive, environmentally friendly house? A number of contestants understood the urban house as both the creature and conductor of the commu-nity in which it sits, however the house is articulated, and that it always includes a necessary proposition about neighborliness. There was a certain amount of wrestling with this, with teasing out the limits of the morphological in amending the social. I was particularly taken with several schemes that looked at least to the scale of the block, keying in shared systems of space and use—whether technical or social. These included water management, collective agriculture and energy production, and community facilities like schools and libraries, as well as propositions about internal circulation and other clear articulations of a semipublic realm for intimate styles of socializing.

Perhaps more surprising were the number of entries that took the "house" problem straight, as a problem to design a single object (figs. 6 and 7). To be sure, in light of the rigorous environmental content of the schemes, it could be argued that all answered to the demands of

a larger global community. But given the irresistibly framed characteristics of this particular community, with its rampant abandonment,
unemployment, income gaps, and educational failures, it did strike
me that the problem could not receive full articulation without some
reference to the next scale up. Indeed, a small number of projects,
described earlier, that did seek to harmonize house and community also
looked to scales beyond that as well. Along these lines, the succinct
analysis of Friedrich Engels in *The Housing Question* of 1872 states a
truth no less true of Syracuse today than of nineteenth-century
Manchester, Berlin, or Paris:

*How is the housing question to be settled, then? In present-day society,
it is settled just as any other social question: by the gradual economic
leveling of demand and supply, a settlement which reproduces the
question itself again and again therefore is no settlement. How a social
revolution would settle this question not only depends on the circumstances in each particular case, but is also connected with much more
far-reaching questions, one of the most fundamental of which is the
abolition of the antithesis between town and country. As it is not our
task to create utopian systems for the organization of future society, it
would be more than idle to go into the question here. But one thing is
certain: there is already a sufficient quantity of houses in the big cities to
remedy immediately all real "housing shortage," provided they are used
judiciously. This can naturally only occur through the expropriation of
the present owners and by quartering in their houses homeless workers
or workers overcrowded in their present homes.*

Engels's argument resonates, particularly in an environment, like
that of Syracuse, in which well over ten thousand homes are vacant
or abandoned. No need to move the food-stamp family into the boudoir
of the bourgeoisie; just turn the key in an unused lock. The core problem
is not architectural but distributive. Indeed, several good submissions
acknowledged this in proposing to literally redistribute housing stock
by moving existing structures into vacant lots and devoting energy
and funds to the renewal of vacant or underused houses (fig. 8).
One submission argued that, one and one-half renovated houses
could be had for the cost of every new one, although it's also true
that many asbestos, lead, and rot-laden structures are better blown
away. Whatever one thinks of the many excellent proposals for new
housing, the context is inescapably one that raises the question of the
equitable access to resources. That this work was produced at the
point of maximum catastrophe in our present housing crisis, with its

Design Cannot Solve This Problem.

Fig. 5. Statement by
Atelier Mobius

Fig. 6. Ackert Architecture /
Dunne and Markis /
Hood Design's entry

Fig. 7. APTUM Architecture's
Up[lift] House

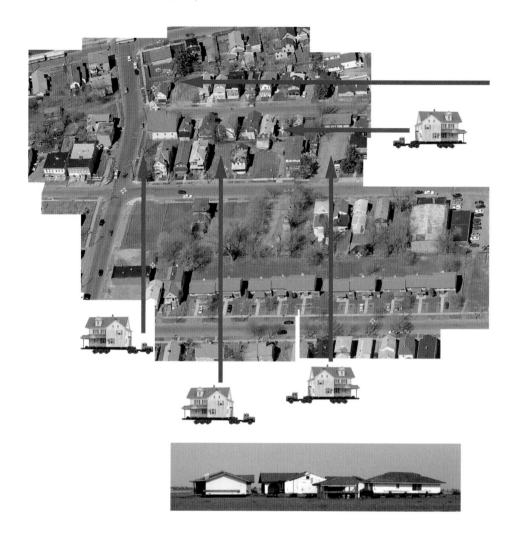

Fig. 8. AGPS Architecture's proposal
for redistributing housing stock

rampant foreclosures and toxic financing, only fixes the issue
more clearly.

Engels's aside about the old city/country chestnut also finds a fresh
context in this work. It isn't just that Syracuse is an exemplar of a dev-
astated proletariat, a town that industrial work has long abandoned,
but that so many of the projects submitted have an agrarian strain and
embody a fantasy about new unities of town and country, striving for
little domestic autarchies—patches of self-sufficiency in a landscape
of dependency. For me, this embodies the best kind of optimism, and
a raft of projects striving for the independence of self-help and mutual
aid is surely tonic.

Family Values

A single-family home proposes a certain predicate: it is to be the home of a single family. But this "product" is obsolete: the nuclear family is now a minority arrangement in the United States. Of course, a "house" need not formally match a family: all kinds of things might go on in those four bedrooms! But a number of submissions went beyond the competition brief to insist that some aggregation was indispensable. These ranged from local connections between adjoining houses, to various multifamily configurations, including AWAKE Architects' Big Ole Sturdy House (fig. 9), combining two to seven dwellings in semicommunal arrangement—an idea strangely missing from the submissions as a whole. A more common critical variation on the single-family container was live/work houses. Nice idea, of course, when there are jobs.

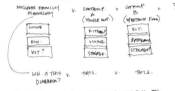

Yard Work

A classic genre of American domestic expression, the yard was approached from all angles: *privacy* as barbecue, ornamental garden, car-repair compound, or some other scaled-up social space. Everyone was obliged to wrestle not only with design particulars, but also with the meaning of this disaggregated green—the encapsulation of "nature" into fungible moments of property. This is a mood that's out there. A week doesn't pass without another proposal to renaturalize Detroit or Queens. A number of suggestions, such as Workscape's consolidated Backyard Farm (fig. 10) and Fiedler Marciano Architecture's Freedom Lawn (fig. 11), proposed a reaggregation of this resource for collective use. Way to go. The ambivalence of the yard is a marker of the tension between private and public and, especially, of the degree of subsidy required to sustain suburban disaggregation with its self-indulgent densities and distances.

A Swale Time Was Had by (Almost) All

The current signifier of environmental sensitivity is the swale (fig. 12). It is clear from this compendium that never again will Syracuse be troubled by runoff, nor its aquifer threatened with depletion! Swales are legible biological networks that visibly perform a vital role in the urban system. They are also models of a genuinely synthetic system, one that works on water conservation, water quality, sewer overload, CO_2 sequestration, harvestable biomass, and heat-island mitigation. And they are scalable, constructible natural systems. The swale offers the possibility of forming big networks of micro-interventions, at once satisfying

Fig. 9. AWAKE Architects' Big Ole Sturdy House

Fig. 10. Workscape's Backyard Farm

Fig. 11. Fiedler Marciano Architecture's Freedom Lawn

the ethic of voluntary aggregation and tackling a problem that ramifies
at giant scale.

Plain Decency

The idea of the low-cost house in the poor neighborhood begs a certain attitude toward modesty, or gives at least an opinion about the
location of the sumptuary. Many of the proposals are clad in a winning
and foursquare style of austerity (fig. 13), a precision of details meant
to evoke, surely, the moral and economic rectitude of the Shakers on
the one hand and the factory on the other (channeled through exem-
plars like Buckminster Fuller or Moshe Safdie). Despite instructions
to eschew manufactured processes dependent on the production of
multiple dwellings, a number of competitors insisted that the mating
of scale and economy embodied in the mass-made house was central
to sustainable practice—and they may be right (fig. 14).

A Little Strangeness

Of course, others bridled at the idea of visual stricture and looked
to various strategies to make their schemes at least passing strange
(fig. 15). The repertoire included encouraging numbers of eccentric
shapes, vertical greenery, and a recurrent whiff of John Hejduk to
charm the eye.

Native Forms

There's a certain inescapable circulation between righteousness
and kitsch, the nativity of oneness with the planet, with the wisdom
of the ancients. I was taken back to my own architectural youth by
certain solutions—the sod houses, the fabulous off-the-shelf Unadilla
Silo Company product, the tweaking of indigenous stick-stylings, the
Iranian wind catchers. There's something of incredible value here: the
idea that the wheel already works damn well. The future of architecture lies not in further technicalization, but in deploying what we've
known well for ages. Why spend millions on gas-filled, highly insulating
glass when you can simply open the window?

Intrusions in the Earth

Several womb-y schemes burrowed into the earth (fig. 16) or at least
sought to heap sod on the rooftop in Great Plains style. The arguments
are a little diffuse, mostly a thermal and back-to-nature gloss. But
there is a certain cultural suggestiveness that grows from a sense of
breakdown, of structures contoured to some vague apocalypse. Here
there's the idea that we revert to Cormac McCarthy troglodytes, that

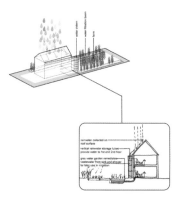

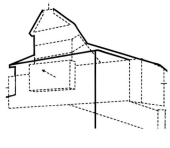

Fig. 12. Burr and McCallum
Architects' rainwater conservation
and reuse strategy

Fig. 13. Za Studio's foursquare
adaptations

Fig. 14. Workshop/apd's
preliminary ideas

perhaps a return to the earth will render us inconspicuous to the rov-
ing zombie hordes, evoking too a certain nostalgia for that fixture of
our greatest suburban era—the fallout shelter. There's also an idea
about remaking the city in a way that's alien from virtually every way
we think about it, almost each of which embodies some version of the
heavy lay on the land.

Good Stuff

We recently moved into a new apartment, one that had been done
up with fine brand-name appliances, just like the ads. After years of
no-name landlord specials, we were thrilled to have crossed over the
borderland of branding, to be at swim in this pool of excellent privi-
lege. Perhaps, in part, under the baleful influence of LEED, many of the
submissions included spec-like *lists* of the righteous environmental
appurtenances and technologies that would be included in the built
project. As a kind of inclusionary mantra this makes a kind of sense:
PV, clivus, superinsulation, reused lumber, windmill…ommmm.
There is something appealing about the shift in our readiness to
ornament and include in our work a raft of ready-made signifiers for
righteous behavior, for the performative, not merely the symbolic.
I take my dog-eared copy of the *Whole Earth Catalog* down from the
shelf and am delighted at this return of the repressed.

Core Values

I was again brought back to my own formation via ideas of low-tech
interventions in areas of despair, means of turning around the squatter
settlements that were such a beau ideal of progressive architecture in
the day. The notion was of forms of accretive intervention, providing
that architectural sand grain that would produce the pearl of sound
and happy habitation. The large number of projects in this competition
that suggested new technical cores and clip-on services surely moved
in the stream of light, but were also provocative interventions. This
seems a crucial principle, allowing the transformation of existing stock,
attuned to the Home Depot style of self-help, a way of self-improvement
with real cultural chops—permanent help with throwaway visuality.

The Moralism of the Model Home

As Gwendolyn Wright, among others, has discussed, the idea of the
model home has long been a medium for propagandizing the family,
the role of women, the nature of correct domestic behavior, and
various other moral imperatives of bourgeois culture, via the profes-
sionalization of the design and provisioning of housing. What are the

Fig. 15. LOT-EK's neighborhood plan

Fig. 16. Cadwell Murphy's earthwork
strategies

ethical/structural desires behind these new projects? Certainly the small-increment social unit, the family as default (with the possibility of substitute forms), comprises the map that these projects trace with little question. There is not much argument for "superior" alternatives, not much experiment, not even much gesture toward such familiar possibilities as cohousing or deeper forms of communalism.

Most interestingly, though, the folks who actually wound up buying these houses *were* exceptions to the waning rule of the family of four. One house went to a single, working mother, another to a childless, semiretired white couple, a third to a newly gotten-together multi-cultural couple. They were, perhaps, drawn to the pride of structures outside old norms. This seems to be an extremely important—perhaps central—role of progressive architecture: to provide forms of comfort that match the desires of a far wider array of forms of affinity than the market cares for.

This reasonable scalar and conceptual reticence (the competition was for a house, not the reconstruction of society) extends, as noted, to larger ideas of community, to the way in which this potential piece of social sourdough is embedded in its neighborhood, to modeling it. The probable contribution lies not in the physical architecture of the house, nor in any generalization of the specific social structure to inhabit it. Rather, these projects are dominated by architectural incite-ments to "sustainable" lifestyles and hypothesize a community of values focused on the maximum use of self-produced energy, disciplined habits of consumption designed to reduce waste and recycle what there is, a willingness to till for one's supper in the garden, and to wrap the house in the signifying apparatus of environmental rationality.

Help Yourself

More than a few projects included the participation of their occupants in the work of actually designing and building. Sweat equity is a literal buy-in, and the idea of inhabitant wisdom—especially if the inhabitants are wise members of the working class—gives a special sanction to the politics of the project. The conundrum comes in matters of form. This was an architectural competition and the obvious prejudice was for an encapsulated work of architecture. In this territory, the winning idea is not in the particulars of any single house, but in the expansion of an accessible repertoire of choices. The risk: too tailored, too specific. The hope: many more ways of building well.

But if choice for the ill-housed is truly the goal, it must also be asked: what would they do with a generous voucher? A fair but misleading question. Housing "choice" has always been a masquerade for the project of throwing the poor into the street. The achievement of this competition has been, first, to insist that neither the homogenizing model of the rundown welfare state nor the cruel exclusions of the Republican market fetish can solve a problem in which quality and diversity must be ineluctably joined. This crucial persuasion is met with a second crucial assertion about what the multiple publics that comprise our society actually share. It is both obvious and bold to insist: the planet. From the Ground Up enriches the repertoire of delightful answers to a central question of the age.

BUILT HOUSES

R-House
Architecture Research Office
and Della Valle Bernheimer

Live/Work/Home
Cook+Fox Architects

TED House
Onion Flats

Photographs by
Richard Barnes

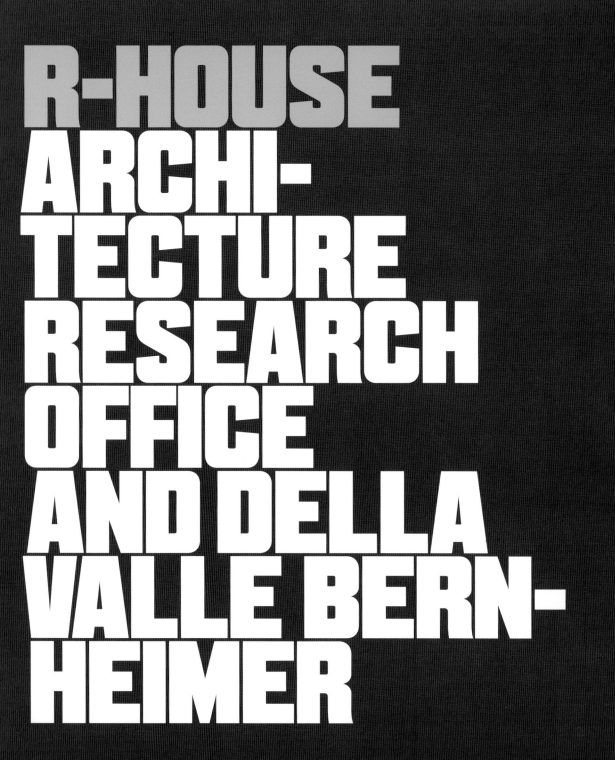

R-HOUSE
ARCHI-TECTURE RESEARCH OFFICE AND DELLA VALLE BERN-HEIMER

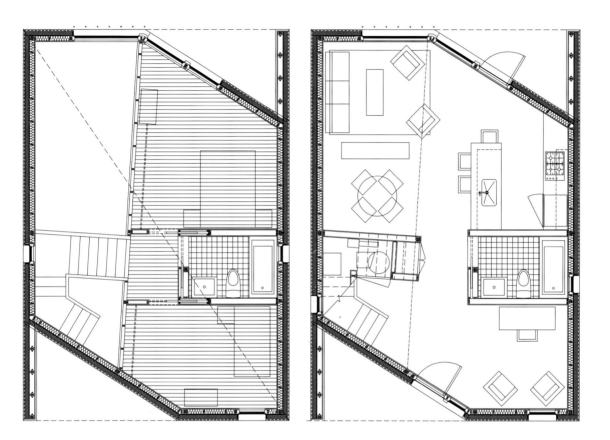

First and second-floor plans

Previous page: Street view

R-House is the prototype residence created by Architecture Research
Office and Della Valle Bernheimer for the 2008 competition From the
Ground Up. We joined forces for From the Ground Up to leverage
each firm's separate expertise and our prior experience as a team;
Architecture Research Office and Della Valle Bernheimer have designed
numerous private residences and other projects independently, and in
2007 we completed our first collaboration—an affordable housing
project for East New York. Subsequently, we worked together on a
very large mixed-use tower for the Hudson Yards area of Manhattan.

Near Westside neighborhood
with proposed R-Houses used
on multiple infill sites

Designed using German Passivhaus principles, R-House is an affordable, innovative paradigm for minimal energy consumption in a home.
The name of the project comes from the R-value—a unit of thermal
resistance that measures the thickness of the material divided by its
thermal conductivity. When spoken, the "R" becomes "our," connoting
the design as both a product of our effort and a home belonging to the
person who lives in it.

Precipitous Times
It is possible now to reflect on R-House as a product of the times
in which it was designed. From the Ground Up began in September
2008 before the fall of Lehman Brothers, and we submitted the
project one month after the presidential election. As our work on
R-House progressed, it was very evident that the country and the
profession of architecture, including our individual practices, would
be affected by an economic recession unlike anything previously
experienced during our careers.

From the Ground Up asked us to reinvent the American house at the
height of the mortgage crisis. Home prices were falling; energy prices
were climbing; homeowners were defaulting on their mortgages.
The central economic asset in the lives of many Americans seemed
hopelessly jeopardized. Syracuse, the site of the competition, had
not experienced the boom or bust of recent times. The Near Westside
neighborhood was emblematic of Syracuse's long economic decline,

as well as its emerging potential. A dedicated group of stakeholders organized this national competition to imagine new possibilities for the city and its inhabitants, and achieve tangible results. As Architecture Research Office and Della Valle Bernheimer surveyed the social and physical landscape, we agreed that for Syracuse and the United States, true sustainability had to be economic sustainability.

Development of R-House

How many designers does it take to create a 1,100-square-foot, highly energy-efficient house?

Major projects at both Architecture Research Office and Della Valle Bernheimer had been canceled or put on hiatus suddenly. Neither firm had yet made staff cuts, so our team for the competition was much larger than it might have been under other circumstances. Over a dozen designers were in the room at our first joint meetings. With this abundance of staff, we were able to assemble a body of research that encompassed a broad range of information, including environmental conditions of the site, the character of the neighborhood, and the Syracuse real estate market. We had a clear sense of the local context and the budgetary constraints of the project right away.

We held weekly brainstorming sessions and design meetings during the tight timeframe of the competition. These sessions were a proving ground for both established and new ideas, as we sought to integrate sustainable practices into an affordable house. We quickly developed a catalog of strategies for responsible environmental design, but we came to a consensus early on that these strategies had to be coupled with a building system rooted in common sense. The house had to be straightforward and logical to construct. The team also decided that any system for construction or for life-cycle functionality had to be free of the costs and risks associated with cutting-edge technologies or equipment. This suggested a Passive House, which was a proven way of building that had been widely implemented in Germany and elsewhere in Northern Europe.

The Passive House standard fulfilled our goals and satisfied the diverse attitudes toward green architecture represented within our team. Once we had oriented our work in this direction, we invited Transsolar to consult with our team. While at Transsolar and later through his own firm Right Environments, David White was an energetic and knowledgeable collaborator from initial design through completion of

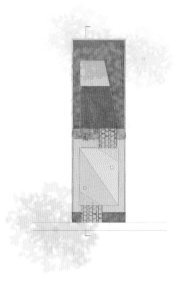

Above:
Site plan

Opposite:
Wall section

construction. We learned the fundamentals of Passive House during design, developing our ideas for the house while at the same time building a body of information on the high physical and mechanical requirements necessary for the required level of performance. David showed us that the standards adopted in Europe, though seldom used in the United States, were very applicable in Syracuse. He provided several examples of constructed homes, so our trepidation regarding the applicability of the Passive House standard was allayed at the outset. Using special software developed by the Passive House Institute, David also modeled the performance of many design variations to verify if our design would meet the stringent standards for energy performance.

In addition, our research revealed that American families waste considerable sums of money each year on high utility bills because of the poor energy performance of the status quo American home. And we were surprised to learn that in Europe there were thousands of certified Passive Houses, while in the United States there were only about a dozen. We became convinced that learning to build better, in a manner that meets the Passive House standard, could help create green jobs in America. This might begin to transform the building industry while reducing our nation's dependency on fossil fuels and ultimately helping to mitigate climate change.

Architecture Research Office and Della Valle Bernheimer worked independently and in joint critique sessions to evaluate numerous design alternatives and focus our efforts, which involved multiple plan iterations, 3-D diagrams, and many physical and digital models constructed by both offices. We were energized by the goal of finding the ideal form that united efficient space planning with high-energy performance. It was through our models that the final form of R-House came into focus. Our brigade of designers created dozens of study models in a variety of materials to envision R-House. The culmination of this work was the half-inch scale model that was a required deliverable for the final presentation.

Sheep in Wolf's Clothing

To express the level of performance and the spirit of our design, Della Valle Bernheimer found an image of a woolly sheep standing in a field. We thought of R-House as a sheep in wolf's clothing: comfortable and cozy on the inside, sleek and modern on the outside.

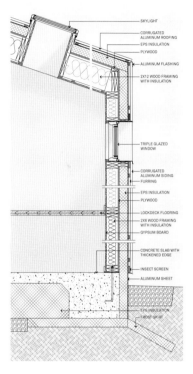

Street view, rendering

Living room, rendering

R-House's walls are 16 inches thick and filled with blown-in fiberglass insulation. Heating the house through a Syracuse winter consumes the same amount of electricity as a hair dryer. R-House utilizes an extremely well-insulated exterior, airtight construction, and limited fenestration to achieve a steady interior temperature. Minimal heating and cooling is provided by a single mechanical unit that quietly circulates air throughout the house. This design reduces R-House's electrical consumption by approximately 70 percent compared to a typical Syracuse home.

The design is as compact as possible on the exterior to minimize energy loss through the envelope, and as large as possible on the interior to maximize the sense of space and light. After exploring many possible forms and massing, we developed an angular, sweeping roof that recalls the gabled rooftops and scale of Syracuse's Near Westside homes. We found that this shape also optimizes Passive House performance. The fenestration captures south light all day. Walls and roof are sheathed with corrugated aluminum, whose silver color, muted reflectivity, and fine texture contribute to a sense of vibrancy that counters the gray winter months.

The interior of R-House is airy and bright. Lit by large windows that open to a view of the backyard, a two-story space on the south side of the house is bounded by the stairwell and the master bedroom on the second floor. Strategically placed windows provide views of the outside from throughout the interior. Through humble, carefully detailed materials—such as concrete, wood floorboards, and plywood panels—the house is imbued with warmth and integrity. Within an essentially open layout, the plan establishes clear boundaries between the different program areas of the house.

As an affordable housing prototype, R-House has a plan that flexibly accommodates a variety of living situations, from a single person to a childless couple to a traditional or extended family. R-House also offers the possibility of being subdivided to create a rental unit. Especially in the Near Westside housing market, this rental income would provide even greater financial sustainability for its owner. The layout can be easily adapted for different sites and solar orientations as well. The design's versatility, durability, and superior energy efficiency, achieved through the simplicity of form and modest materials, make R-House a vital means of building a resilient community.

Under Construction

Although it occurred over a much longer timeframe than the competition, construction of R-House was equally intense. While the home is constructed with wood members and familiar framing systems, the geometry of the project and its stringent air-infiltration requirements meant that there was a steep learning curve for the builder and carpenters. Exterior walls that are typically made with 2-foot-by-6-foot wood studs were framed instead with vertical TJI beams. These I-shaped members are usually used on horizontal installations, so joinery was more complicated than usual. All joints in the exterior envelope required nearly perfect sealing from the outside air, so taping details were highly prescribed both at windows and at sheathing panels. Windows are triple-glazed and argon-filled, and their installation had to be impeccably executed—they were potentially the single biggest source of air infiltration in the house.

Near the end of construction, the airtightness of the house, which is much higher than that of a typical American home, was measured with a "blower door test." A fan was attached to the front door, and the interior pressure was differentiated from the air pressure outside. An assessor walked around the home with a smoke stick while the fan was running. This helped identify the exact locations of weakness in the envelope so adjustments could be made. When the leakage was reduced to a proper level, no more tests were needed, and the house achieved infiltration levels appropriate to the standards of the Passive House Institute. Full Passive House certification for R-House is in process with the Passive House Institute and is expected within the coming months.

Pioneering a Resilient Community on the Near Westside

The process of designing and constructing R-House was an incredible opportunity for our team to put forth a new model for Syracuse's Near Westside neighborhood. We believe that the goal of sustainable housing shouldn't be merely to reduce CO_2 emissions, but to advance the financial security of individual American families and communities. Design excellence in this context demands affordability by reducing both short-term construction costs and long-term energy-consumption costs. We hope that R-House and the other two projects built "from the ground up" present a compelling paradigm for cities across the country willing to rethink their housing priorities in the recession's wake.

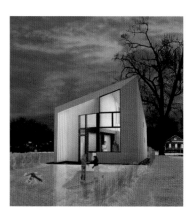

Rear view, rendering

Model

Following pages:
Rear view with TED I louse,
rear view; side view; bedroom;
living room; street view

I had a hard time affording my suburban house as a single mom. I don't want that life ever again.

Homeowner Maggie Maurer

In the fall of 2010, along with her boyfriend, Peter Waack, Maggie Maurer, a Building Performance Institute certified building analyst and single mother of three, purchased the R-House.

Team Credits

Architecture
Architecture Research Office: Stephen Cassell and Adam Yarinsky, principals; Megumi Tamanaha, associate; Melissa Eckerman, Jane Lea, Neil Patel, and Anne-Marie Singer, design team

Della Valle Bernheimer: Andrew Bernheimer and Jared Della Valle, partners; Garrick Jones, associate; Lara Shihab-Eldin and Janine Soper, design team

Landscape Architecture
Coen+Partners: Shane Coen, principal

Climate Engineer
Transsolar: David White, senior engineer and project manager

Structural Engineer
Guy Nordenson and Associates Structural Engineers: Guy Nordenson, principal; Brett Schneider, associate

Estimator
Stuart-Lynn Company: Breck Perkins, principal; Daniel Edelstein and Denis Vasin, team members

LIVE/WORK/ HOME
COOK+FOX ARCHITECTS

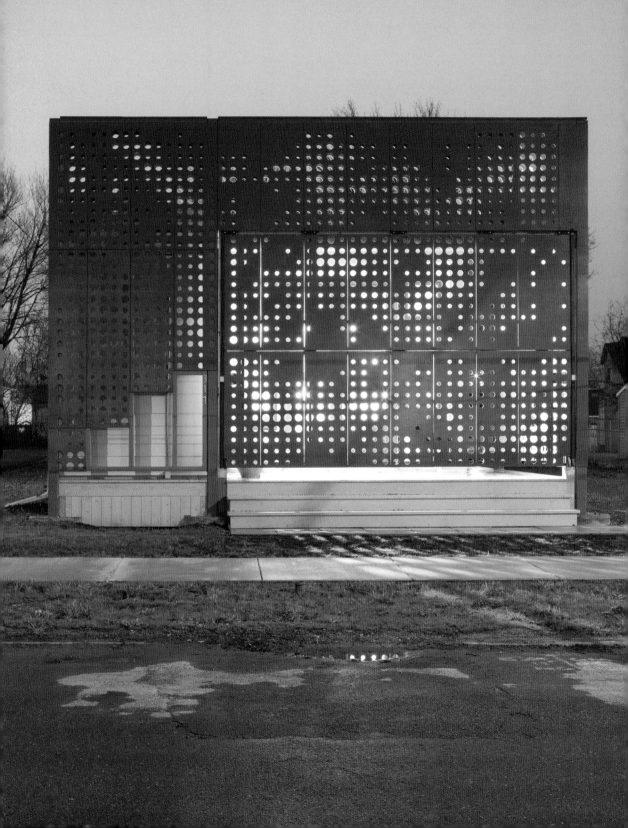

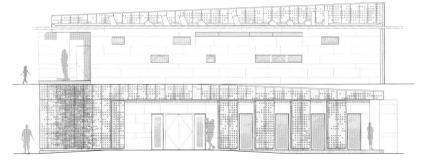

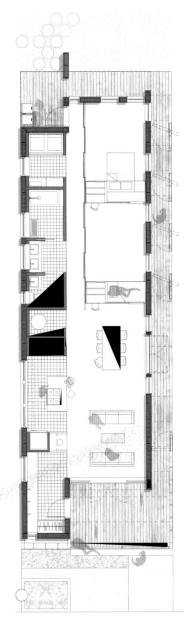

Left:
First-floor plan

Above:
Rear, street, and side elevations

Previous page:
Exterior at night,
privacy screen closed

Our approach to the From the Ground Up competition stemmed from reconsidering the definition of "home" within the context of the Near Westside: a neighborhood in a shrinking postindustrial city. As each of us draws from his or her unique and individual life experiences, it was important to reevaluate our assumptions about "home." I personally came with a world view developed from growing up during the 1960s and '70s on a suburban cul-de-sac in New York. Our neighborhood was a place solely reserved for "living," and each day the parents—typically the dads—started up their cars and drove to a place called "work."

My experience as a first-time home buyer was fundamentally different. My wife and I purchased a former worker's cottage on an aging industrial waterfront, where I was surrounded by wildly divergent living and working patterns. In fact, I was the only person in this urban neighborhood who followed the traditional pattern of traveling to work in the morning and home at night. The separation of the realms of live and work is a notion that is clearly outdated and due for consideration as we attempt to rebuild our neighborhoods for longevity and respond to the problems created by decades of suburban sprawl. As Buckminster Fuller once said, "Our beds are empty two-thirds of the time. Our living rooms are empty seven-eighths of the time. Our office buildings are empty one-half of the time. It's time we gave this some thought."[1]

As our team came to understand the Near Westside, which has been plagued by high unemployment rates and vacant lots following the loss of major manufacturing plants in the twentieth century, we quickly realized that the last thing the neighborhood needed was another single-family home. Instead, the area desperately needed work: its vitality is a question of sustaining livelihoods and the social diversity that makes a community.

Our ideas about sustainable, long-term growth strategies for the Near Westside were influenced by the legend of the Three Sisters, a planting method pioneered by the Haudenosaunee, in which corn, beans, and squash were considered "inseparable sisters" that thrived when interplanted. The legend reminds us that biodiversity and interdependence are essential to healthy human systems; like our natural ecosystem, successful communities flourish with diversity. Live/Work/Home seeds the neighborhood with a building typology that is specifically designed to add mixed uses and drive a positive cycle of long-term investment in the community.

With its flat-roof profile, Live/Work/Home is stripped of the iconography of traditional residential architecture and instead is just as easily associated with commercial building typologies. As we began to rethink the rooted concept of home in this particular time and circumstance, we aimed to spark diversity of building types to encourage further mixed-use development.

As a prototype, this response is widely applicable and intended for replication within varying contexts and areas; in essence, the Near Westside functions as a case study for this type of flexible design, which could be reiterated and tweaked for different settings across the nation. Rather than focusing creative, economic energy on the edge of the neighborhood, the design builds off a strategic infill approach that reinforces the fine-grained lot structure of the neighborhood.

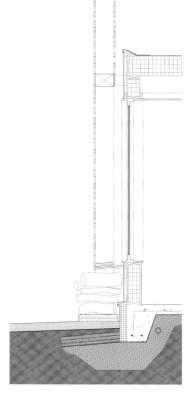

Detail of wall section

However, due to the extremely low land values, some recent development projects in the area combined sites using lot mergers. Reinstating the original density of the neighborhood is vital for forming social connections within the neighborhood. This intervention will mix residential and entrepreneurial activity fluidly within a single site. We envisioned Live/Work/Home functioning as a home-based small business or artist's studio that easily converts to suit a family with children, an extended family unit, or a student household. The unique flexible qualities of the space—essentially a small modern loft—could attract new residents and uses, helping to repopulate the urban neighborhood, while being rooted in the vernacular of the area and equally attractive to long-term residents as a new home.

The building's simple design is based in highly efficient planning, and includes a consolidated service core and a large, open loftlike area for living, working, and sleeping. We also designed a system of mobile casework furniture that simultaneously creates bedrooms, achieving the greatest possible flexibility at the least expense. While dozens of configurations are possible, we studied seven generations of plan

development, including student bedrooms and an intergenerational
family's sleeping accommodations. Likewise, instead of two standard
bathrooms, disaggregated bathroom components serve more people
in less space. The exterior screen is also infinitely adaptable to different owner identities, privacy preferences, or site orientations, with
perforated panels that can be repositioned or replaced with alternate
patterns and materials. Because it is multifunctional at many scales,
Live/Work/Home allows for a lifetime of waste-free remodeling along
with the do-it-yourself affordability of a loft.

Our interest in minimizing waste throughout the project moved beyond
setting up an aggressive target for construction-waste diversion—
we looked to reuse as many available materials as possible. Materials
from two local deconstruction projects were salvaged for repurposing: wood from the home previously sitting on the site became flooring
in Live/Work/Home, and wood from a nearby warehouse was reused
as kitchen cabinetry.

The long, narrow site suggested an exploration of linear typologies,
including the Charleston Single and the Haudenosaunee longhouse,
Syracuse's original vernacular form. Live/Work/Home's one-story
structure, while not the most economically or energy-efficient form
in a cold northern climate, is an easily adaptable layout suitable for
a broad range of residents, allowing the owners to "age in place,"
promoting intergenerational living. The neighborhood has seen
a significant decrease in residents of the older generation, diminishing
demographic diversity; we felt strongly about addressing this trend
with a design that would breed neighborhood unity and familiarity by
encouraging long-term residence.

As a firm, our work is shaped by a fascination with ideas around healthy
living and biophilia—our innate human need for connection with the
natural world. We believe that buildings can be designed to reinforce
this connection to nature; as social ecologist Stephen Kellert says,
"Without the positive benefits and associated attachment to buildings
and places, people rarely exercise responsibility or stewardship to
keep them in existence over the long run."[2]

The design directly responds to Syracuse's climate and ecology:
the city experiences long, light-starved winters, in which daylight hours
in January fall 30 percent below the national average. Though presented with a difficult, north-facing site orientation, the building

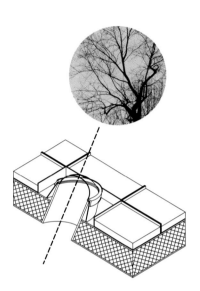

Detail of skylight tube

is placed to maximize solar exposure, lit with direct and diffused daylight from skylight tubes penetrating the roof. The skylights protrude at varying heights from the roof, providing a light source that removes the constructed barrier between the indoor and outdoor environments and varies according to day and season as snow heights morph light patterns on the floor. Occupants will remain attuned to the outdoor environment in the midst of winter. Again, Kellert speaks on the restorative effects of daylit spaces: "Natural light is both physically and psychologically rewarding to people…the benefits of natural light are often enhanced by modulating daylight. Filtered or diffused sunlight can also stimulate observation and feelings of connection between spaces, particularly inside and outside areas."[3]

Exterior in winter and autumn, renderings

On the exterior, a perforated screen wrapping the western and northern facades bounces daylight onto the north-facing porch, and filters or reflects evening light through adjustable rotating screens along the western side. Few things touch on the beauty of the pattern of dappled light filtering through a tree canopy. Although many patterns could be used for future iterations of the structure, we were inspired by this particular natural phenomenon when designing Live/Work/Home. We drew from Janine Benyus's research on biomimicry, a related field to biophilia, which teaches us about taking design cues from nature. Benyus writes, "This is where biomimicry finds its nexus with biophilia—where structures derived from natural principles wind up reminding us of life-forms around and within us."[4] Part of the screen, a large garage-type front door, can fold down to create a secure, open-air anteroom; when open, this space engages the sidewalk and the street like the vernacular front porch, instilling awareness and an ethic of "eyes on the street" that help residents feel safe and in touch with ongoing neighborhood activities.

Given the strict project budget, our goal was to build a structure that operated at a minimal ongoing cost despite rising fuel prices. Considering long-term operational affordability during the design process was especially important when addressing the needs of aging residents and students. Low-tech passive strategies became the foundation of the home's green design concept and affordability. A simple but well-insulated building envelope constructed from structural insulated panels (SIPs) saves energy, improves comfort, and reduces both material waste and the total cost of ownership. SIPs are high-performance building panels custom designed with precut openings for windows and doors. We chose them for their ultimate material efficiency and ease of construction; because they travel in simple flat packs for on-site assembly, SIPs remove the inefficiency of "shipping air" associated with transporting more voluminous, preassembled homes, while still benefiting from the minimized construction waste and higher quality control of factory fabrication. An added advantage was the education that the installation team received, instilling a knowledge base of an unfamiliar building material and process within the local labor pool.

Cross-ventilation and a heat recovery ventilator with CO_2 sensors circulate healthy filtered air year-round. During hot summer evenings, the garage door can be closed, allowing front doors to remain open for additional ventilation and natural cooling while maintaining privacy and security. The roof is covered with a single-ply high-albedo membrane, a reflective coating that will lower the absorption of solar energy and decrease heat transfer into the home—an additional cost-saving measure. Efficient low-emissivity insulating glass windows exceed Energy Star requirements. Beyond affordability, our concern with building for longevity and physical sustainability meant creating the healthiest indoor environment for owners. Materials were chosen to protect the indoor air quality by reducing the risk of moisture, mold, and the off-gassing of harmful chemicals.

Local nonprofit Home HeadQuarters managed the construction process, which included training for a team of construction apprentices, cultivating a workforce for future sustainable building projects, and creating much-needed green-collar jobs.

Although the residents of the three completed From the Ground Up projects have lived in the space for a short time, we hope that these insertions have spurred new conversations in the existing neighborhood that continue beyond the excitement during construction. We are interested in the stories that all three new houses weave within the existing fabric of the Near Westside as thoughtful interpretations of the local architectural vernacular and also as studies of the American shrinking city.

Following the end of the jury process, community member Carole Horan remarked, "I went back to the neighborhood where I've been living for thirty-seven years and looked at it with new eyes, paying more attention to details that I had never noticed before. My fondest wish for this neighborhood and, indeed, the whole community is that we all look with new eyes."

Above:
Flexible interior as artist's space, living space, and office space, renderings

Following pages:
Exterior shade panels; detail of privacy screen; living space; stairs to basement; dining area; living space, with bedroom at left; view from front porch; exterior at night, privacy screen open

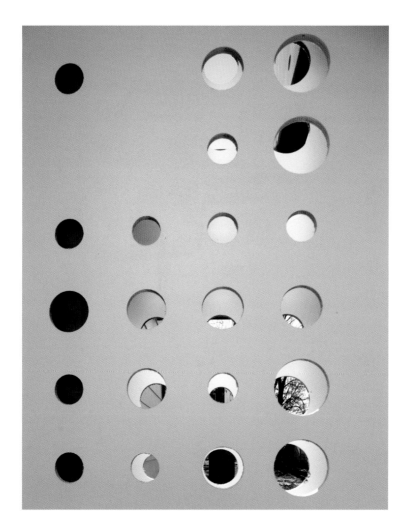

We totally love being here. It's beautiful. It more than fulfills our aesthetic standards; in fact, it way exceeds my aesthetic standards. It's brilliant.

Homeowners John and Kathy Miranda

John and Kathy Miranda, a semiretired couple, purchased the Live/Work/Home at the tail end of the construction process. The Mirandas moved to the Near Westside from an apartment in downtown Syracuse.

Team Credits

Architecture
Cook+Fox Architects
Rick Cook, partner; Ilija Bentscheff, Tyler Caine, Pam Campbell, Mark Canfield, Simone DeConno, Guido Elgueta, Alice Hartley, Brandon Hendricks, Zoe Logan, Fred Metzger, Simon Rearte, Eugene Sun, Caroline Hahn, Dan Brammer, and Nina Roefaro

Environmental Consultant
Terrapin Bright Green
Bill Browning and Chris Garvin, partners

MEP Engineer (Competition)
Arup
Nigel Nicholls, principal; Kristina Taylor

MEP Engineer (Project)
Jaros, Baum & Bolles
Tim Fu

Structural Engineer
Severud Associates
Edward DePaola and Andrew Mueller-Lust, principals; Fortunato Orlando, Matthew Peitz

Landscape Architecture
Terrain-NYC
Steve Tupu, principal

Sustainable Construction Consultant
Northeast Green Building Consulting
Kevin Stack, principal; Josh Stack

1   R. Buckminster Fuller, *I Seem to Be a Verb* (New York: Bantam Books, 1970), 175.

2   Steven Kellert, Judith Heerwagen, and Martin Mador, *Biophilic Design: The Theory, Science, and Practice of Bringing Buildings to Life* (Hoboken, NJ: John Wiley & Sons, 2008), 11.

3   Ibid., 244.

4   Janine Benyus, "A Good Place to Settle: Biomimicry, Biophilia, and the Return of Nature's Inspiration to Architecture," in Kellert, Heerwagen, and Mador, *Biophilic Design*, 33.

Section elevations (top) and
plan diagrams demonstrating
flexible layouts

Previous page:
Exterior, rear view

*Our proposal for this single-family 1,100-square-foot home, affection-
ately referred to as TED, focuses on a dwelling that both challenges
and supports the project's historic Near Westside neighborhood.
TED was conceived as a prototypical home that could comfortably sit
on a variety of lots in the neighborhood and yet be unique to each site.
Programmatically, TED is surprisingly versatile, easily transformed
from a two- to a three/four-bedroom home, into two duplex units,
or into a home office/studio with residence above, all accomplished with
minor interior alterations. A small addition to the rear of TED creates
the option for future expansion. TED is a dense, ultra-efficient, thick-
skinned, yet light-filled and spacious powerhouse of contemporary
urban dwelling. TED exudes more energy than it consumes, collects
and recycles water, and has the ability to produce food. TED easily
meets the LEED for Homes Platinum Certification requirements.
Its form follows function pleasingly, as the lines of the gables rise
in direct and perpendicular relation to the equinox sun, creating a
mechanism for both heating and cooling, naturally and sustainably.*

As the introductory text for our proposal to the competition, it's an
astonishingly accurate description of the home as it was built—
astonishing mostly because we completely redesigned the home after
we won the competition. Considering the combination of alterations
by the owner, like the addition of a basement, and our own changes, it's
surprising that TED even came close to the budgetary intentions of the
competition. Why the hell would any architect in their right mind enter
a competition to design a highly sustainable home to be built in the
middle of a nondescript and forgotten neighborhood in Syracuse,
New York, and have it designed and built for $150,000? We knew that
we'd spend as much time on this little house as we would on a project
ten times its size. We also knew that with the budget specified, this
wasn't a project of fetishized detailing, but rather one in which each
detail had to function in at least three ways if it were to make the cut.

If the budget for the competition had been a more reasonable
$250,000, we probably wouldn't have entered. It was precisely

the challenge of the budget that held our attention, because as a company we've been posing for years the same questions provoked by the competition, ones similarly posited by early modernists about the inspirational power of architecture (and, within this century, net-zero-energy architecture) for the masses, not just the elite.

If there was a reason TED even came close to its lofty intentions , it was because of one person, Mike Hughes, the construction manager for Home HeadQuarters and TED. One of our first encounters with Hughes was when we told him we were going to completely redesign the envelope of the building just as zoning permits were being issued. The summer before construction started, we took Passive House—certification courses in New York City and were obsessed with TED becoming our Passive House guinea pig. Our competition proposal prided itself on a "conventionally framed" house, "well" insulated with R-19 batts in the walls and R-30 in the roof. After our Passive House training, we were embarrassed by such a wimpy shell. We told Hughes we'd stay within the budget but needed to now build a superinsulated (R-44 in the walls, R-52 in the ceiling), airtight building, capable of achieving net-zero-energy status. He smiled warmly and encouraged us to develop the idea further. Given the fact that Hughes was working on several (at one point I think he said twenty-five) projects simultaneously, he should have told us to grow up and stick with the original plan, as such a significant alteration could never work within the budget. But he didn't. He fully supported our hubris as we went from a 2-foot-by-6-foot wall with batt insulation and R-1 windows to a 2-foot-by-6-foot wall with closed-cell spray foam, dense-packed cellulose, zip-panel air barrier, 4 inches of EPS rigid insulation on the exterior, a metal panel rain screen, and R-10 windows. We found a recycled rigid-insulation supply company that sold, to our amazement, "used" XPS and EPS panels at a fraction of the cost of new. We thought we had discovered the holy grail of Passive House products. (We actually entertained dreams of becoming a distributor for the company!) In reality, though, about 50 percent of the panels delivered had been so abused, torn, and tattered when they were wrenched from their previous lives that they were not merely useless but a liability. Hughes entertained experiments such as these without judgment, as he was genuinely committed to testing new and cost-effective ideas for making this house, knowing that some simply wouldn't work, but some might.

In the end, the extra time, work, and money spent on the envelope paid off: it enabled us to reduce the cost of the mechanical equipment,

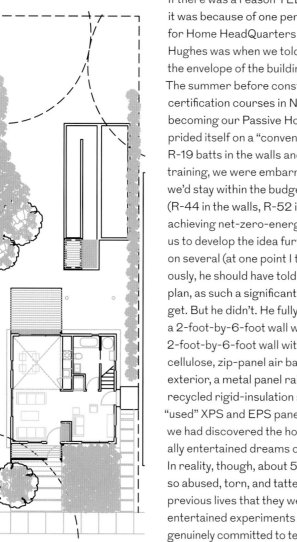

Site plan

Dining area and living area, renderings

gave us a virtually airtight shell, and allowed us to reach the most difficult requirement of a Passive House building. In the blower door test, TED measured 142 cubic feet per minute at 50 pascals, a result equaling 0.45 air changes per hour at 50 pascals. (Passive House minimum requirement is 0.6 air changes per hour at 50 pascals.)
This is a very difficult number to achieve and is five times more airtight than the LEED Platinum home we recently completed in Philadelphia. What it means is that TED has the equivalent of a fur coat, rather than a windbreaker, standing between it and the harsh Syracuse winter. It also means that the heat generated from within stays within and requires very little heat to actually be generated.

Cooling was an entirely separate but related issue. The form of the home in general is informed by the three-story open-interior atrium space within. This combined with the climate of Syracuse eliminated the need for mechanical cooling during the summer months, and so none was installed. Natural convection created by this carved-out form creates a "solar chimney," continuously exhausting warm air and humidity from the home while maintaining a comfortable ambient temperature inside.

As our attention focused more critically on a Passive House— influenced thermal envelope, our initial strategy toward heating, cooling, hot water, and mechanical systems in general completely changed with it. Within the "wimpy shell" period of TED's evolution, we pre- ferred, both conceptually and financially, the mechanical technology that generates heat over the building science that both holds it in and

Street view, rendering

radically reduces the need for it. Initially TED was envisioned to be donned with four 6-by-6-foot evacuated-tube solar thermal panels located on the 44-degree sloped, south-facing roof combined with a 120-gallon storage tank capable of providing close to 100 percent of the heating and hot water needs of the home. Backed up by a high-efficiency condensing boiler and in-floor radiant heating through-out, a robust solar engine (and with it a robust price tag) became the beating heart of TED. TED effectively took the money devoted to this "active" solar engine and put it into the "passive" building envelope. Heat and hot water requirements are still met with a high-efficiency condensing boiler and in-floor radiant heating, and with the future addition of two 6-by-6-foot evacuated-tube panels, 100 percent of the heating and hot water requirements would be met by the sun. With the further addition of a small array of photovoltaic panels in the previously proposed roof area, TED's net-zero- or even net-positive-energy aspirations would likely be achieved.

Energy was obviously a significant focus of TED. It occupied the majority of the design and building team's time and resources. Consequently, other areas of commitment initially promised by

TED languished. Stormwater management and landscaping were two of the biggest losers. While the majority of the site remains pervious, given TED's small footprint, none of the more active stormwater collection strategies—such as a 1,000-gallon underground rainwater cistern, or rain garden, prominently located in the front yard that would have managed rainwater from the entry-porch roof and walkway while hosting a community of native, flowering plants that would have attracted pollinators—survived the final months of the dwindling construction budget. Particularly disheartening was the absence of any of José Alminana and Andropogon Associates' tantalizing and cost-effective landscape design projected in our initial submission:

Native and fruiting trees require no irrigation and provide texture, shade, and scale to the front and rear yard, while producing food and supporting the local wildlife. In th e hearty side yard, "Red Sprite" (Winterberry) shrubs produce gorgeous red fruit that will remain on the branches long after the leaves have fallen, enhancing the winter landscape and enticing songbirds....All turf is a "No Mow" lawn mix, which blends six different deep-rooted, drought-resistant fescue varieties.

While none of this happened, TED still, surprisingly, achieved its intended LEED Platinum status. All that was missed in the process can still occur in the future with the new owners, who appear to have all of the requisite pride and responsibility of new and excited parents. In order for TED to be all that it can be, it will need the vision, determination, and potential that only good parents can foster in their children. And so TED's life has only just begun. We're proud of TED's accomplishments to date and are eager to witness a more mature growth. We remain engaged in that growth by having recently submitted to Home HeadQuarters our designs for TED2, to be sited a few blocks away from TED, with a cedar-shingled rather than a metal-clad skin. And while TED2 may have the benefits of the collective failures and successes of TED behind its design, and therefore ostensibly claim the title of a "better TED," we will forever reserve a warm and endearing place in our hearts for the original, in all its incompletion, the inimitable TED.

Above:
Model and rear view, rendering

Following pages:
Detail of third-floor loft; basement; view from loft to living space below; kitchen from above; view into loft; kitchen; street view with R-House

Our house is cheaper than our apartment was— and it's a thousand times nicer.

Homeowners Steven Morris and Sara O'Mahoney
Steven Morris and Sara O'Mahoney purchased the TED House in late 2010. Syracuse housing provider Home HeadQuarters helped the young couple, who also own a bicycle shop in the city, get down payment assistance and tax incentives.

Team Credits

Architecture
Onion Flats: Timothy McDonald, Howard Steinberg,
Pat McDonald, John McDonald, Ted Singer, Jim Sanderson,
and Linda Montanile-Smith

Landscape Architecture
Andropogon Associates: José Alminana, Patty West,
and Darren Damone

Energy Consulting
MaGrann Associates: Dave Bone and Sam Klein

Structural Engineering
Rivera Structural Design: Amy Rivera

FINALISTS

Asymmetric House
Adjaye/Associates

Insular House
Office dA and Studio Himma

Otisco House
do-it-together

Lumen-Air House
Erdy McHenry Architecture and
Stenson-Building+Furniture Design

ASYMMET-
RIC HOUSE
ADJAYE/
ASSOCIATES

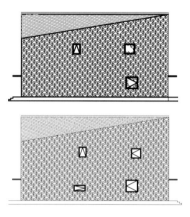

Above:
Side elevations

Right:
First- and second-floor plans

Previous page:
Model

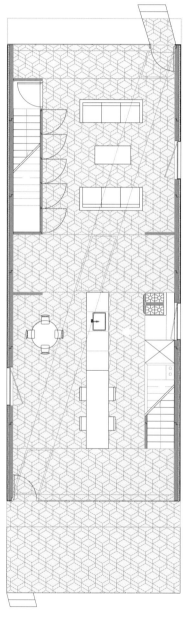

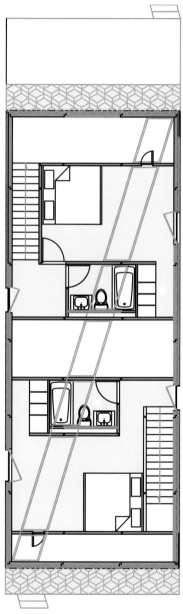

We have progressed in recent years technologically and are coming to grips with years of environmental damage; yet, our lifestyles, our regulations, and our housing stock, by and large, remain unchanged.

As we begin to identify a concept, we take into consideration that as a city Syracuse has been suffering both financially and demographically, with industry leaving the area as well as a 30 percent decline in population over the past fifty years. Neighborhoods are being vacated and house prices are dropping.

Additionally, Syracuse is infamously known for one of the most polluted lakes in the United States—Onondaga Lake. Hundreds of millions of dollars have been dedicated to curbing the ongoing damage to the lake and its surroundings, declared a Superfund site since 1994, due to industrial waste. Toxicity from nearby industrial production has poisoned the lake with high levels of chloride, sodium, and calcium, and the lake continues to be damaged by treated wastewater.[1]

Lastly, we also understand our climatic challenges of warm summers, cold winters, and amazingly abundant snowfalls.

We propose Asymmetric House.

Asymmetric House is a hot coal in the snow, a version of a log cabin crafted of large structural timber panels on a tile-concrete base. As a country, we are known for making heat, but we are less known for retaining it. Through its construction, this house seeks to be both a heat and cool sink by absorbing heat throughout the winter and letting it radiate inward.

Our structure is a 9-inch-thick solid timber wall. Wood is one of the most effective materials for storing heat; it stores two times that of concrete. Timber makes up the bulk of the envelope as a structure, as a temperature mediator, and as a finished wall surface.

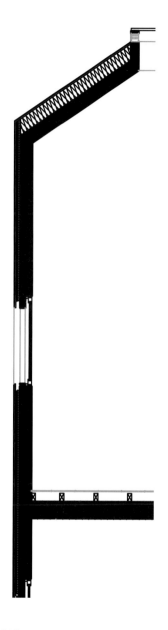

Wall section

Outside the wood structure, we wrap the building in insulation to keep moisture out of the house (and reduce the possibility of mold) and protect it with a layer of clay tile. We use clay for both its thermal and biodegradable characteristics and its low cost.

The building shape is informed by traditional gabled-roof house types. It departs from conventional form with a monolithic structure system and lighting strategy, making a very open space and directing daylight to all parts of the house through a ridge of light, as well as allowing expansive openings toward the street and yard.

Passive heating strategies, which absorb radiant heat from the sun and exchange heat or cold from the earth, determine the choice of materials of tile, concrete, and wood.

We believe that the comfort provided by a warm, efficient, and bright structure enhances a sense of security and hominess and promotes a sense of ownership in the house and the community.

Asymmetric House seeks to limit the use of fertilizers, artificial light levels, labor, water use, energy used for heating, and toxicity in building materials.

The house reduces its environmental impact in a variety of ways: it eliminates fertilizers through plant selection; utilizes the ground as heat exchanger, heating and cooling the structure; maximizes daylight with strategic skylighting within the building form; minimizes water use by collecting rainwater; reduces toxin levels by minimizing interior finishes; and maximizes energy storage through the thermal mass of floor, walls, and ceilings. Asymmetric House also works to develop stronger social ties by minimizing labor costs through prefabricated construction, opening the social aspects of the house to the public realm.

Improvements to the Framed House

Thermal Mass
Solid timber panels are the walls and are considered mass walls. Timber also forms the ceilings of the project. Concrete-slab floors provide a robust surface for everyday life and also allow heat from radiant floors to disburse evenly throughout the space

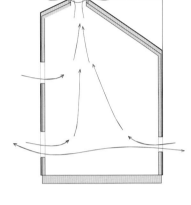

Above:
Ventilation diagram

Cross-Cut Laminated Timber Panels

Prefabricated CNC-milled cross-cut laminated timber panels substantially minimize erection time and provide both structure and thermal mass, as well as a timber-box interior finish, allowing the timber to be appreciated for its performative and aesthetic values.

Radiant Hot-Water Heating

Using a closed-tube heat-exchange system, the house creates a passive radiant system in which water is heated by absorbing the sun's radiation, reducing fossil fuel dependencies.

Daylighting

Departing from conventional window openings, skylights along the ridgeline can provide daylight throughout the house, reducing the need for artificial light.

Ground-Source Heat-Transfer Radiant-Floor Heating

A slinky, or underground, closed-loop heat-exchange system can provide an alternative to conventional oil and gas boiler systems by working with the earth's ambient temperature to provide heat during the winter and cooling during the summer months.

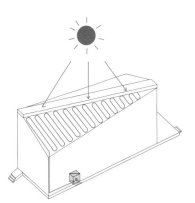

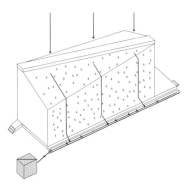

Above:
Solar heating system;
storm-water system

Following pages,
clockwise from top left:
Exterior view in winter;
kitchen; exterior view; model

1   Upstate Freshwater Institute, "UFI Home," http://www.upstatefreshwater.org.

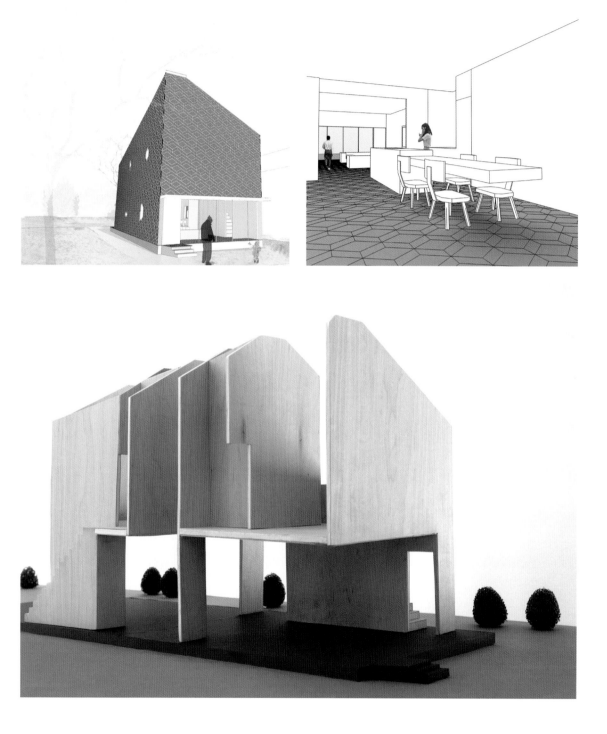

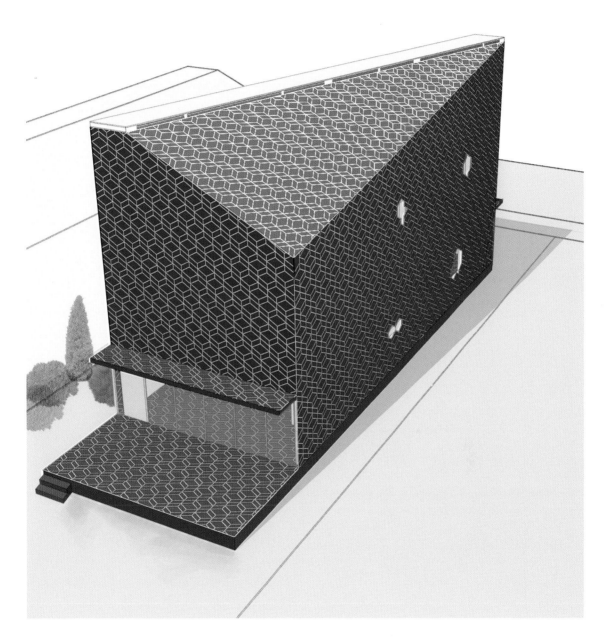

Team Credits

Architecture
Adjaye/Associates
David Adjaye, principal

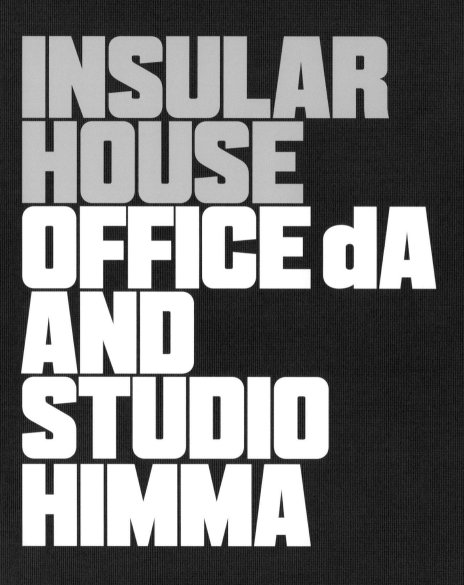

INSULAR HOUSE

OFFICE dA
AND STUDIO
HIMMA

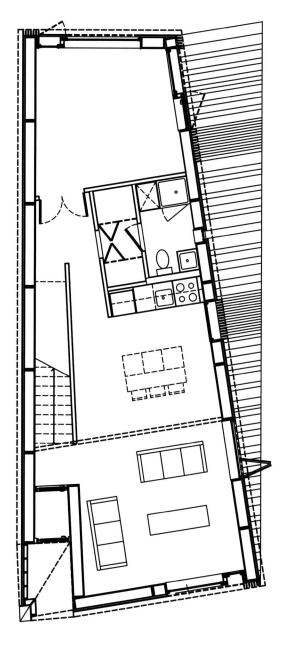
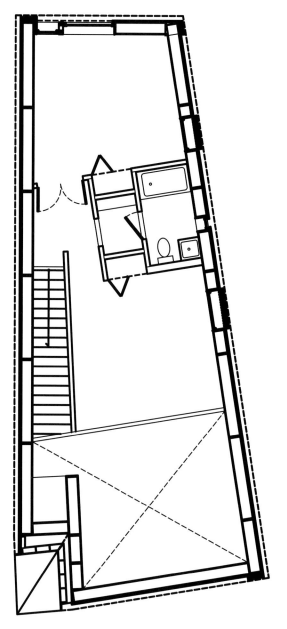

Above:
Side elevation

Opposite:
First- and second-floor plans

Previous page:
Exterior, street view

Of the challenges posed by the From the Ground Up competition, the economic one is the most pressing, especially under strain by the requirements of sustainability; any normative house would breach the allotted budget without effort. For this reason, our proposal argues for radical economies, couched precisely in sustainable terms, as a way of integrating certain fundamental goals. The techniques we adopt are unorthodox, though they ultimately use planning, massing, and material strategies that make the dumb box "smart."

To this end, the house is planned around some basic principles: a simple foundation, straightforward massing, and an interior that is gauged toward flexibility. The strategy is to minimize construction complexity, eliminating multiple trades, materials, and assembly processes. Thus, the foundation is a slab-on-grade with a structural insulated panel (SIP) wall and roof system. The slab-on-grade minimizes excavation costs while also producing thermal mass. The SIP wall and roof system overcomes the multiple layers that normative construction is encumbered by, instead creating a thick insulating wall. In combination with the natural ventilation, this is perhaps the most effective way to reduce energy use: minimize life-cycle costs while reducing the construction costs up front. The roof has a single slope, using all the water runoff for site-water sequestration. Beyond these principles, we have worked with a set of varied strategies, attempting to make a project that is more than the sum of its parts. Thus, we evaluated the field of materials and selected those that can serve a building's function in its entirety, be fabricated regionally if not locally, and adopt an assembly process that is efficient enough to minimize waste and lower costs. Finally, our attempt has been to wring as much architectural benefit out of these select few materials without sacrificing their inherent efficiencies.

Instead of a house of smaller square footage and a higher finish, we have opted for a strategy that offers a spatial distribution that can be used with more flexibility, thus accommodating the kind of flux that characterizes the evolving American family. In this way, we can scale our house from 1,300 square feet all the way to 2,000 square feet: first, as a more open house of two bedrooms; second, as a variation of the first with an open loft in the living area; third, as a three-bedroom house, with the option of an internal expansion within the double-height living area to achieve four bedrooms; and fourth, as a home office on the ground level, with the possibility of two or three bedrooms upstairs. The idea is that the house can evolve over time as families grow or decrease in size and respond to shifts in the economy. Ultimately, the argument is to treat the housing stock as social infrastructure, imagining that its sustainability is linked to its ability to transform over time and serve the community by accounting for the growth of families, shifts in real estate, and changes in work/living habits.

Improve: Simple, Green, Practical

The house is designed in simple ways not only to reduce the use of energy during construction, but also for its overall life-cycle costs. The design strategy also ties the house into large-scale economies by evaluating and designing with the fewest number of materials and processes while harnessing a high level of performance, both technically and aesthetically.

Slab-on-Grade
The first floor is located on grade using an insulated-edge concrete slab. By isolating the earth under the home, the heat/cool cycle is tempered. The concrete slab itself acts as a thermal battery, holding on to warmth or coolness when required.

Superinsulated Building Envelope
By greatly slowing the rate of heat loss or gain between inside and out, the project eliminates the need for conventional heating and cooling. Heat given off by equipment and people within the space warms the house in winter (in addition to the solar heat load through windows), and the exposed slab cools it in summer.

Heat Recovery Ventilator
Working in tandem with the superinsulated shell, the heat recovery ventilator maintains indoor air quality (through ventilation and filtration) and retains up to 85 percent of the energy otherwise lost to the mixing of outdoor and indoor air temperatures.

Evacuated-Tube Solar Hot Water Heater
An average of 40 percent of electrical expenditures in U.S. residences

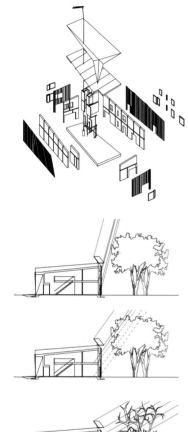

Exploded axonometric
and sun/shade study

go to heating and cooling water. Capturing the radiation of the sun on precisely oriented panels and using that heat (in lieu of electricity, gas, or oil) can provide up to 75 percent of the home's hot water, or even more with an expanded panel.

Roof/Rain Garden Site-Water Sequestration
The dual slopes of the site and roof act to channel water to native plant-ings, which percolate the water, allowing it to gradually filter into the ground. This benefits both the owner and the community by enriching and cleaning the soil and groundwater and reducing stress on munici-pal systems, especially the local combined sewer.

Exterior Cladding
As older agricultural buildings in Onondaga and neighboring counties become decommissioned, their weathered old-growth wood siding is salvaged and reused. The project takes advantage of the superiority of reuse over recycling by utilizing the variable width of these old boards in multiple ways—as siding, louvers, and doors.

Value: The Neighborhood and the Construction of a Community
It is hard to make designs for a single house that affect an entire com-munity, but if one imagines a system that can operate in broader terms, then its economies will be felt at the larger, public scale. To this end, beyond a proposal for a house, we offer an interpretation of the project that can have an impact on the entire land owned and being developed by Home HeadQuarters (HHQ).

Water Retention
The first idea is to keep water that arrives on site, on the site itself. This reduces strain on the area's combined (storm water and sewage) sewer system, lessening long-term municipal costs. Current systems (overflow catchments) depend on steady or decreasing stresses to prevent overflow of raw sewage into rivers and onto streets. Given the scope and ambition of HHQ's current and planned holdings, this is a strategy whose effects would multiply across greater areas, and one that already has both the support of Onondaga County leaders and a legislative funding proposal pending.

Landscaping
The second idea is to plant natural native grasses that can clean local air and soil—as compared to lawns, the fertilizing of which contributes to lower water quality and decreased fisheries (11 percent of

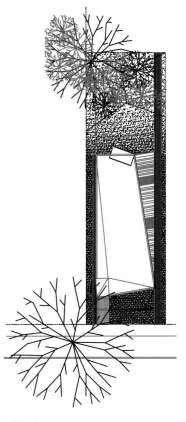

Site plan

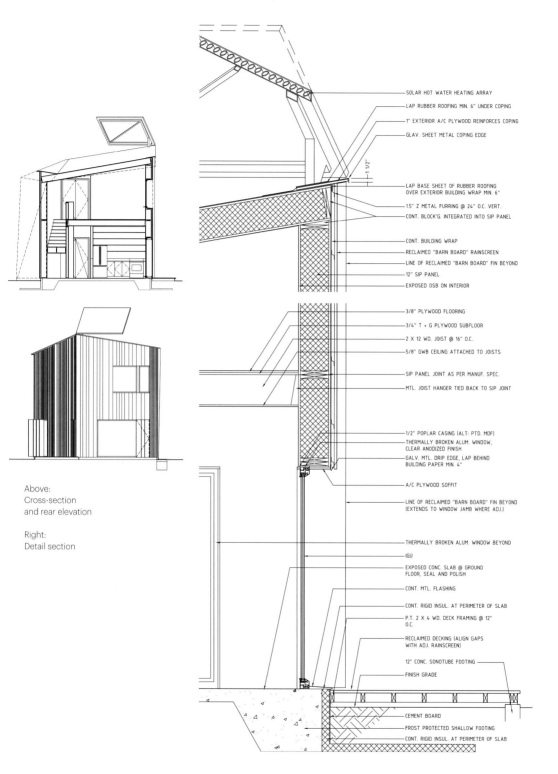

SOLAR HOT WATER HEATING ARRAY

LAP RUBBER ROOFING MIN. 6" UNDER COPING

1" EXTERIOR A/C PLYWOOD REINFORCES COPING

GLAV. SHEET METAL COPING EDGE

1 1/2"

LAP BASE SHEET OF RUBBER ROOFING
OVER EXTERIOR BUILDING WRAP MIN. 6"

1.5" Z METAL FURRING @ 24" O.C. VERT.

CONT. BLOCK'G. INTEGRATED INTO SIP PANEL

CONT. BUILDING WRAP

RECLAIMED "BARN BOARD" RAINSCREEN

LINE OF RECLAIMED "BARN BOARD" FIN BEYOND

12" SIP PANEL

EXPOSED OSB ON INTERIOR

3/8" PLYWOOD FLOORING

3/4" T + G PLYWOOD SUBFLOOR

2 X 12 WD. JOIST @ 16" O.C.

5/8" GWB CEILING ATTACHED TO JOISTS

SIP PANEL JOINT AS PER MANUF. SPEC.

MTL. JOIST HANGER TIED BACK TO SIP JOINT

1/2" POPLAR CASING (ALT: PTD. MDF)

THERMALLY BROKEN ALUM. WINDOW,
CLEAR ANODIZED FINISH

GALV. MTL. DRIP EDGE, LAP BEHIND
BUILDING PAPER MIN. 4"

A/C PLYWOOD SOFFIT

LINE OF RECLAIMED "BARN BOARD" FIN BEYOND
(EXTENDS TO WINDOW JAMB WHERE ADJ.)

THERMALLY BROKEN ALUM. WINDOW BEYOND

IGU

EXPOSED CONC. SLAB @ GROUND
FLOOR, SEAL AND POLISH

CONT. MTL. FLASHING

CONT. RIGID INSUL. AT PERIMETER OF SLAB

P.T. 2 X 4 WD. DECK FRAMING @ 12"
O.C.

RECLAIMED DECKING (ALIGN GAPS
WITH ADJ. RAINSCREEN)

12" CONC. SONOTUBE FOOTING

FINISH GRADE

CEMENT BOARD

FROST PROTECTED SHALLOW FOOTING

CONT. RIGID INSUL. AT PERIMETER OF SLAB

Above:
Cross-section
and rear elevation

Right:
Detail section

pesticides used in the United States come from grass fertilizers), and the cutting of which consumes 800 million gallons of gasoline per year, producing 5 percent of all air pollution in the United States.

Mutual Reinforcement: Size and Flexibility
Third, the house provides a flexible framework for long-term and variable habitation, accommodating residents' full life-cycle use requirements. The construction methodology allows for expansion and encourages adaptation as lifestyles and demographics change. This flexibility is capable of supporting a lifetime resident: a single person or young couple, one to three children's rooms, and a single-floor living area for empty nesters and seniors. This has the added benefit of encouraging long-time occupation, a key to self-sustaining investment at a community level, enhancing the importance of long-term residents to the immediate neighborhood. Neighborhoods prosper when people start making more money (e.g., get older, get promotions, etc.) and remain stable in their location.

The Intersection of Sustainability and Economy is Locality
By purchasing materials and paying for fabrication as locally as possible, both economic and environmental costs are reduced. Our preparatory research sought out companies and products with established and efficient means of providing high-value products: SIP producers across New York State, aluminum products potentially recycled at the Oswego Novelis plant, and salvaged barn siding from Onondaga, Cayuga, and other adjoining counties. Though the project is a small contribution in and of itself, as exemplar it serves notice that regional sourcing is an economical and sustainable option, even in Central New York's ever more postindustrial service-based economy.

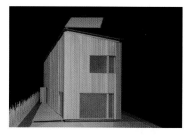

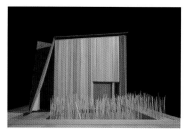

Above:
Street view in winter; model, rear view; model, street view

Following pages:
Interior view; street view; side view; interior view of stairway and second floor

Team Credits

Architecture

Office dA

Nader Tehrani, Monica Ponce de Leon, Dan Gallagher, Jeff Dee, Arthur Chang, Harry Lowd, Brandon Clifford, Jessica Colangelo, Lisa Huang, Rich Lee, Catie Newell, Kazuyo Oda, Narijus Petrokas, Remon Alberts, Suzy Costello, Melissa Harlan, Adam Fure, and Ellie Abrons

Studio Himma

Hailim Suh and Jeff Dee

OTISCO
HOUSE
DO-IT-
TOGETHER

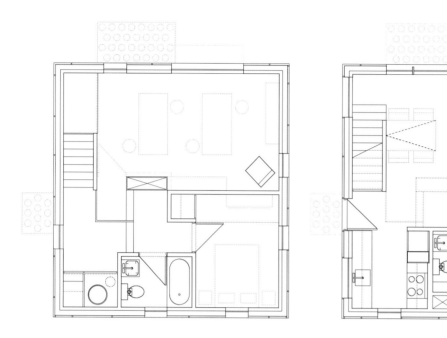

Above:
First- and second-floor plans

Previous page:
Model

The Otisco House is a multilayered, compact volume that touches the ground lightly. The simple exterior envelope contains spaces of varied proportions spiraling around a stair core, producing an inherently flex-ible, energy-efficient house. Openings in the stair core frame vertical and diagonal views between different levels, giving a sense of spacious-ness, allowing penetration of sunlight, and multiplying opportunities for social contact within the family. One opening, a "light chimney" created by the stair, becomes the symbolic center of the house—the new hearth. The functional chimney and furnace of a typical house have been banished, replaced by the I-shaped fresh-air outlets. Passive solar strategies and an energy recovery ventilator capture ample heat.

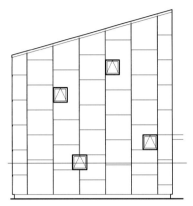

The house is made of thick and thin elements that work together to optimize exchanges and form a resilient structure. Passive House standards have been used to reach design objectives. The super-insulated and sealed envelope creates a constant steady-state environment, while carefully designed openings and overhangs opportunistically engage climate swings. The result is an ultra-simple structure that provides free warmth and light at no additional construction cost.

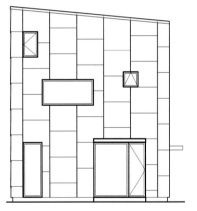

Side and rear elevations

As required by the competition program, the house contains two per-manent bedrooms, two baths, living and dining spaces, laundry, and kitchen. The second-floor "loft" can be programmed in a variety of ways—artist's studio, two children's bedrooms, or main bedroom, with optional demising wall. Interior spaces throughout the house are shaped for different potentials: walls become coves for indirect light-ing, and nooks and ledges can be used for storage, daybeds, or seating.

The house is easily adapted to different sites in and around the Near Westside. The cubic exterior is always oriented toward the sun, while the spiraling interior is oriented toward the front and rear yards. The changing relationship between cube and spiral creates a range of spatial and programmatic types. A minimum of resources produces maximum opportunities.

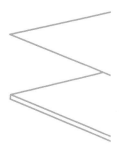

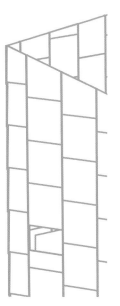

Proposed Improvements

Through Passive House strategies and planning, our house-specific heat demand is only 4.7 British thermal units (BTUs) per square foot annually, 90 percent more efficient than conventional construction.

Active systems strategies include:

1. Energy recovery ventilator. The airtight layer will be tested early in the construction phase with blower door equipment. Because the building envelope is tight, air movement can be easily controlled to ensure uniform ventilation of the entire house. An energy recovery ventilator will control the building's ventilation and capture 90 percent of the thermal energy in exhaust air and recycle it to intake air.

2. Energy-efficient appliances in an efficient core. Energy-efficient equipment and appliances are used throughout. The infrastructure is concentrated to reduce piping and take advantage of adjacencies. While maintaining recommended light levels, the total energy con-sumed for this 1,200-square-foot house is 0.44 watts per square foot (less portable lighting supplied by the homeowner).

3. Rainwater collection. Rainwater is diverted to a water tank, which after five minutes of first flush stores water for gardening, saving up to 50 percent over normal residential water usage.

4. Solar hot water. Clip-on next-generation solar evacuated-tube water collectors provide 64 percent of annual domestic hot water needs.

Passive strategies include:

1. Envelope. The superinsulated airtight envelope maintains constant temperature.

2. Solar gain. Southern openings provide 7,154 kilowatt-hours of heat gain per year. The heat is absorbed in the concrete thermal mass floor.

3. Daylight. Window size, placement, and opening shapes provide daylight throughout the house, even on the cloudiest day in December. Daylight Factors (DF) range from 1.25 DF in the bedrooms to 5.4 DF in the living spaces.

4. Cross-ventilation. Windows are aligned to east and west and posi-tioned to encourage the Venturi effect to take advantage of summer prevailing winds and provide cross-ventilation.

Above:
Exploded axonometric

Opposite:
Active and passive diagrams

Following pages:
Model; view from street

1
Envelope

2
Solar Gain

3
Daylight

4
Cross-ventilation

5
Arrangement of Program

6
Energy Recovery Ventilator

7
Energy Efficient Appliances
in an Efficient Core

8
Rainwater Collection

9
Solar Hot Water

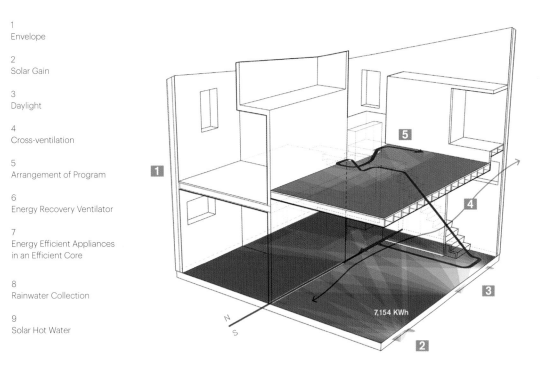

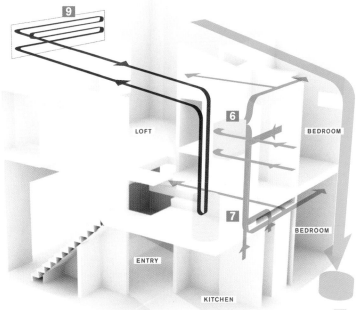

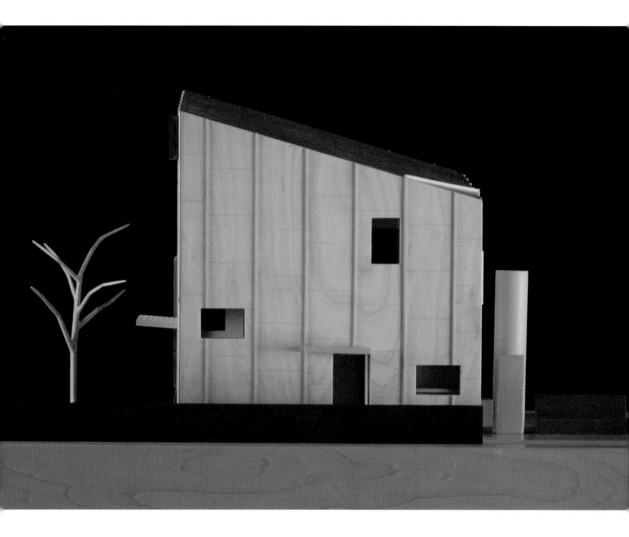

5. Arrangement of program. Centralized circulation provides privacy and easy access to rooms and living spaces, which are oriented to the south, while service spaces are oriented to the north.

Neighborhood Value
The project proposes a new normal—a new way of living for the twenty-first century.

Site Planning
The landscape design for the Otisco House is shaped by internal and external forces, reflecting the interior organization of the house and the needs of the neighborhood. The house sits north of the centerline of the lot and is organized on two stories to optimize useful open space. The front yard invites interaction with the neighborhood. The back-yard is more secluded, with play areas and food-producing planting beds. The roof is pitched down to the north to introduce sunshine into the front yard and along the street. The tallest face of the house, the southern face, permits deep daylight penetration, thermal gain in win-ter, and visual connections between living or loft spaces and gardens. The entrance is located on the east-side wall for privacy. The kitchen is located at the front for security, as the "eyes on the street." Bedrooms, baths, and utility spaces are treated as buffer spaces on the north side. All social spaces face south.

Variation
Variations in massing, siting, program, color, and cladding help the Otisco House fit into the Near Westside, which is characterized by a wonderful diversity of house types. One strategy for design variation, the clip-on system, allows the inhabitant to enhance the house over time with locally fabricated extras. These modifications accommodate changing needs and help the house increase energy independence and sustainability. Some clip-ons, like solar hot water and photovoltaic panels, would also be appropriate for other houses throughout Syracuse. If it obtained funding to train and supervise personnel for these installations, Home HeadQuarters would help build green-collar jobs in the neighborhood. Other clip-ons are simple: most can be built by local tradespeople in a conventional manner.

The clip-on system has advantages over ordinary home improvements, however. It helps owners visualize changes and makes sure they are as green as possible; it presents the customizations as something spe-cial; and it offers a fixed, objective price. Other clip-ons, like proposed spun-metal siding and stabilized-earth landscape block elements, could be locally produced: our team has been in contact with Syracuse manufacturers. The manufacture and installation of clip-ons sows seeds for local economic development.

Team Credits

Architecture

BriggsKnowles A+D: Laura Briggs and Jonathan Knowles

THEM architecture design: Gustavo Crembil and Peter Lynch; Victor Barbalato, Kate Cahill, Jason Lim, and Asami Takahashi, design assistants

Graphic Design

Lisa Maione Studio: Lisa Maione

Lighting Design

Derek Porter Studio: Derek Porter

Passive House Consultant

Passive House Institute us: Katrin Klingenberg, director

Affordable Housing Consultant

Nnenna Lynch

Landscape Architecture

Leonard Newcomb Landscape Architecture: Leonard Newcomb

Mechanical Engineer

Thomas Young Associates: William Thomas

LUMEN-AIR HOUSE

ERDY MC-HENRY ARCHITECTURE AND STENSON-BUILDING+ FURNITURE DESIGN

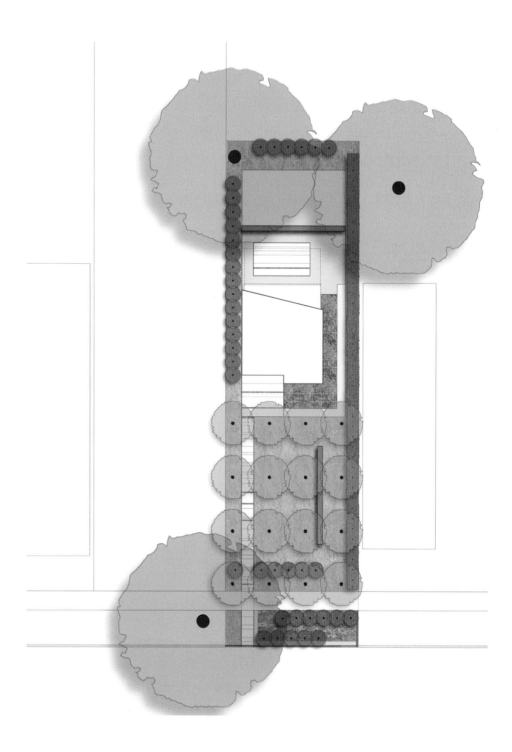

Syracuse's weather poses special challenges to designing high-performing, energy-efficient housing in the city. In August the city is 82 degrees Fahrenheit with a pleasant westerly breeze, but in February temperatures drop to 15 degrees with a not-so-pleasant northwest wind. The challenge is not simply to design a house, but to design two houses in one—a multimode environmental device.

Opposite:
Site plan

Previous page:
Exterior, rear view

The Lumen-Air House is a machine for living, especially living in relation to the weather. In the warmer months (May through mid-October) the house opens like a flower to filter sunlight and accept the free flow of fresh air. In the colder winter months, it buttons up. The interior living spaces are protected and insulated by thermal buffer zones on the north and south faces. Though closed down, the interior of the house glows with diffused daylight through the multiple layers of greenhouse closure. In the shoulder seasons, early-to-mid fall and mid-to-late spring, the open-closed aspect of the house adjusts to the changing weather (snow in May and 65 degrees on Thanksgiving—you never know!). Throughout the year, the Lumen-Air House engages directly and intimately with the weather.

The ambitions motivating the formation of our house as a "weather machine" are threefold. First, we are proposing a design of weather-driven performance. The objective is to radically reduce energy consumption by tapping into the heating and cooling potentials the climate offers when available, and then to close down and conserve when they are not. Our second goal follows directly: reduced energy consumption equates to lower operating costs. This house is cheap to heat and virtually free to cool. Finally, our ambition is to create a house whose outward form manifests an orientation to the weather and the environment. We aim to produce comfort, reduce consumption, save money, *and* tell the story.

In form and attitude, the Lumen-Air House is entirely unlike current housing market offerings. It does not derive its character from a response to the "house-ness" that developers believe the market demands. (This self-fulfilling projection has given us a market choked with oversized, overpriced, energy-gulping houses that are everywhere the same.) As counterpoint, our house celebrates the weather of Syracuse and dwelling in close relation to the climate.

Environmental Systems

The Lumen-Air House is designed to adjust. Its external environmental interface (i.e., its enclosure and ventilating systems) responds to seasonal flows and daily weather fluctuations in order to maintain internal comfort while conserving energy and saving money. Primary environmental systems include passive-first heating and ventilation and thermal buffer zoning.

Sunspace Dynamic Envelope

This zone is formed by two layers of enclosure on either side of a narrow three-story space. A polycarbonate door system and glass/mass enclosure work in tandem to harness and modulate available solar energy. When open, the door system creates overhangs and vertical fins that shade the inner glass and mass layer, preventing unwanted heat gain. The overhead and flanking planes of the retracted doors define the exterior terrace as an extension of the house interior. Closed, the doors form the outer enclosure for a greenhouse space, allowing direct solar penetration and passive heating. This house opens up in the warm weather and then closes up tight for the harsh winter.

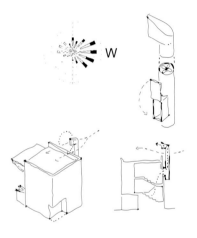

Diagram of
ventilation system

A few feet behind the polycarbonate doors, and angled to face due south, is a wall of precast-concrete tablets and double-insulating glass. During the heating season, the concrete panels absorb daytime solar heat and reradiate this energy to the interior later in the day. The precast panels incorporate circuits of high-density polyethylene tubing that are connected to a ground loop system (associated either with front yard earth tubes or with a backyard stormwater cistern). The coils circulate passively cooled 60-degree water through the panels, dissipating incidental heat gain and providing low-level radiant cooling. Relative proportions of concrete panels and double-glazed walls are optimized to provide thermal comfort and maximum light and views.

Naturally Motivated Ventilation

Our house breathes: it inhales cool air and exhales warm air. Small in plan area, with operable windows on all four sides, the house interior is easily cross-ventilated when outside conditions are cool to warm.

On hotter days, the house still provides its interior with cool currents of fresh air. The stairwell space and ventilation chimney function as a whole-house ventilator. Warm air rises to the top of the tall stair space and is drawn off by the chimney. Primed by the prevailing west winds, the chimney—dubbed "snorkel"—induces a Venturi flow to extract warm air from the house. (An integral fan augments flow when the wind does not provide a strong draw.) Finally, this venting pump can be hooked up to an earth-tube system buried five feet below the north-side front yard. The earth tubes provide cool make-up air and, in concert with the snorkel, circulate fresh, comfortable air throughout the house even during the warmest summer afternoons—air conditioning not needed, not included.

Thermal Buffer Zones

Interior living spaces are separated from exterior extremes by north- and south-facing buffers. During the winter, the sunspace provides an unconditioned, but solar-warmed, layer of air—a light-transmitting, insulating shield. Then, in the summer, this zone opens to exterior air with dappled cool shade provided by the retracted doors. On the north side of the house, the stairwell and service spaces can be closed off from the living spaces and maintained at a lower temperature, providing a winter buffer. Then, come summer, this layer is opened to the rest of the interior and provides cooling ventilation.

We have designed the Lumen-Air House to passively condition itself for half the year and run on passive-active hybrid mode for two more months. Even on active mode, the shelter of the well-insulated envelope and buffer zones results in maximum heating efficiency. Judged against new construction norms, the Lumen-Air House's estimated annual energy savings are between 60 and 70 percent. As energy costs continue to rise, this house becomes increasingly less expensive, relatively speaking, to operate. And, as monthly operating costs shrink, the net-present-value of the Lumen-Air House increases.

Neighborhood Value

The Lumen-Air House does not intend to blend in. On the contrary, our house will introduce a conspicuously positive, yet critical, complement to the character of the Near Westside. The house is optimistic; it outwardly asserts that architecture can efficiently respond to climate and, through design-for-better-performance, provide shelter, comfort, environmental benefits, *and* delight. Through its particular and striking form, we also intend our design to signal, to critically proclaim, that buildings must effectively engage environment.

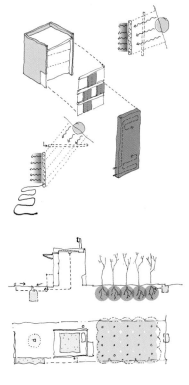

Diagram of thermal massing and diagram of stormwater system

Following pages:
View of house from rear in winter; house in section; bird's-eye view

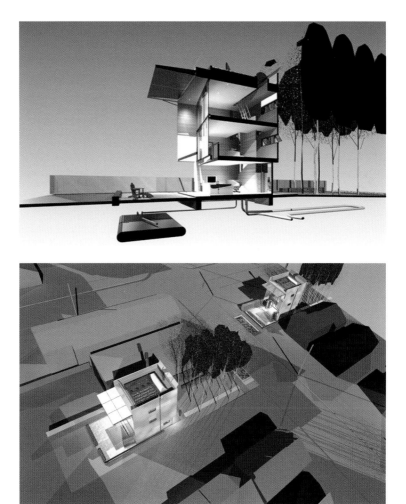

Though not shy, the Lumen-Air House also conforms to and comple-ments the housing fabric of the neighborhood. Volumetrically sympa-thetic with surrounding buildings, our house can patch holes in this fabric. Toward this end, and as there are empty lots on both sides of Otisco Street, the Lumen-Air House is designed to perform equally well in both situations. Should multiple Lumen-Airs be built in close proximity, the apparent solar bias of the house form will generate telling differences between opposite sides of the street. On the sunny south-facing side, the houses will front the streetscape across a shallow forecourt, with operable south walls in full view. On the north-facing side, the houses sit behind a small bosque of birch trees—further back on their lots to insure ample solar access. We offer the potential of this sided difference as an affirming signal inflecting the landscape of the neighborhood to the forces and flows of the climate.

Finally, our project strategy contributes to the landscape of the city as well as to the Near Westside streetscape. The front yards of all north-facing houses are designed to receive the birch tree bosque. Together with green roofs and backyard cisterns, the birch trees process all on-site stormwater. Further, these trees are also "fed" by inlets that divert stormwater from the gutter. Our design goes beyond zero flow into the city's overwhelmed combined sewer system; it actually reduces sewer loading. We propose that most, if not all, empty house lots along Otisco Street be planted with birch trees fed by curb inlets. When it comes time to build more houses, the birch trees can be removed as needed. This sewer-flow-reduction, "green infrastructure" strategy extends the environmental agency of the design from the house to the neighborhood, for the benefit of the entire city.

Team Credits

Architecture

Erdy McHenry Architecture: Scott Erdy and David McHenry, principals

Stenson-Building+Furniture Design: Timothy Stenson

Landscape Architecture

Siteworks

Engineer

AKF Engineers

Opposite:
View into house

SKETCH-
PADS

Applicants interested in competing in From the Ground Up were asked to submit a booklet documenting their qualifications, proposed team make-up, and, in what was called a "sketchpad," preliminary sketches illustrating their initial ideas for affordable, sustainable design in the context of single-family housing.

The following pages feature selections from some of the fifty-two sketchpads submitted, offering a variety of approaches to the social, economic, and ecological challenges present in Syracuse's Near Westside and in neighborhoods throughout America's Rust Belt.

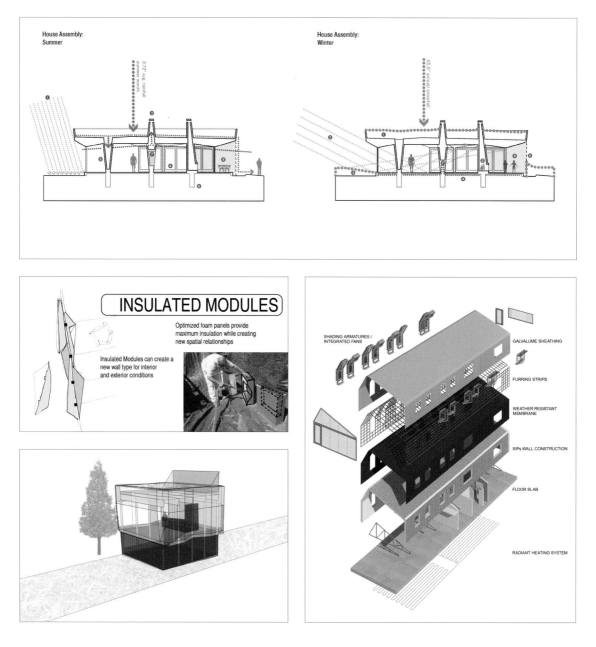

House Assembly:
Summer

3.72" avg. rainfall summer month

House Assembly:
Winter

(15.6" annual snowfall)

INSULATED MODULES

Optimized foam panels provide maximum insulation while creating new spatial relationships

Insulated Modules can create a new wall type for interior and exterior conditions

SHADING ARMATURES /
INTEGRATED FANS

GALVALUME SHEATHING

FURRING STRIPS

WEATHER RESISTANT
MEMBRANE

SIPs WALL CONSTRUCTION

FLOOR SLAB

RADIANT HEATING SYSTEM

Clockwise from top:
PLY Architecture, Ann Arbor, Mich.;
Ackert Architecture / Dunne and
Markis / Hood Design, New York
/ Riverdale, N.Y. / Oakland, Calif.;
Griffin Enright Architects, Los
Angeles

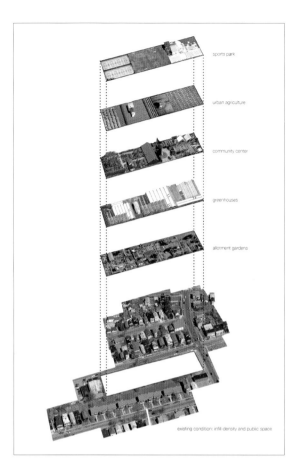

sports park

urban agriculture

community center

greenhouses

allotment gardens

existing condition: infill-density and public space

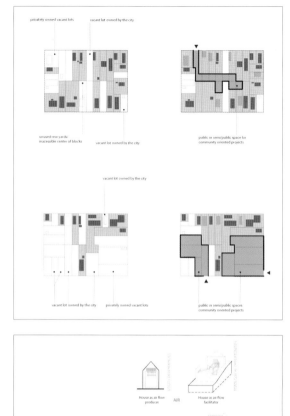

privately owned vacant lots

vacant lot owned by the city

unused rear yards/ inaccessible center of blocks

vacant lot owned by the city

public or semi/public space for community oriented projects

vacant lot owned by the city

vacant lot owned by the city

privately owned vacant lots

public or semi/public spaces community oriented projects

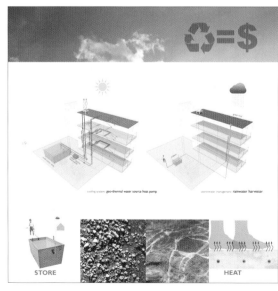

♻ = $

cooling system: geo-thermal water source heat pump

stormwater management: rainwater harvester

STORE

HEAT

House as air flow produce   AIR   House as air flow facilitator

Roof as energy / light container   SKY   Roof as energy / light provider

Ground as Foundation   EARTH   Ground as Buffer

House as Fixture   WATER   House as Distributor

How is energy put to use in architecture? Past terms for energy have been to render it passive. In the process excess energy was wasted. The old model was to control access globally and dispel energy away from the house. The new model is to control energy and release energy at the scale of the house.

Clockwise from top left:
Lang Architecture, New York; AGPS
Architecture, Zurich / Los Angeles;
Onion Flats, Philadelphia;
Studio SUMO, Long Island City, N.Y.

LITTLE GREEN HOUSE

South view

Northwest view

CONNECT>THE HOUSE Southwest view

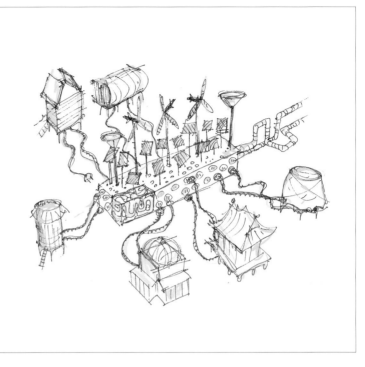

Clockwise from top left:
Digsau Architecture, Philadelphia;
MOTOElastico [Simone Carena,
Marco Bruno], Seoul, South Korea;
Konyk Architecture, Brooklyn, N.Y.; Goshow
Architects, New York; Archi-Tectonics,
New York

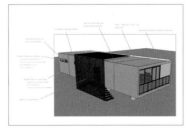

Opposite page, clockwise
from top left:
GAutheir Architects, New York;
MOS Architects, New York;
Studio Luz Architects, Boston

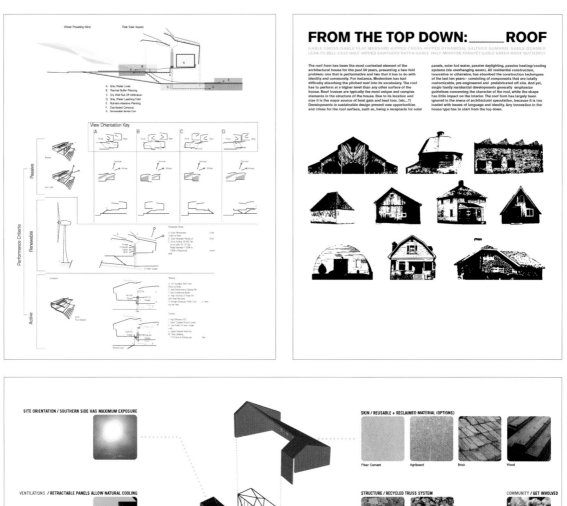

FROM THE TOP DOWN: _____ ROOF

GABLE CROSS-GABLE FLAT MANSARD HIPPED CROSS-HIPPED PYRAMIDAL SALTBOX GAMBREL GABLE-DORMER LEAN-TO BELL-CAST HALF-HIPPED SAWTOOTH DUTCH-GABLE HALF-MONITOR PARAPET-GABLE GREEN-ROOF BUTTERFLY

The roof form has been the most contested element of the architectural house for the past 50 years, presenting a two-fold problem: one that is performative and two that it has to do with identity and community. For instance, Modernism has had difficulty absorbing the pitched roof into its vocabulary. The roof has to perform at a higher level than any other surface of the house. Roof trusses are typically the most unique and complex elements in the structure of the house. Due to its location and size it is the major source of heat gain and heat loss. [etc...?] Developments in sustainable design present new opportunities and crises for the roof surface, such as, being a receptacle for solar panels, solar hot water, passive daylighting, passive heating/cooling systems (via overhanging eaves). All residential construction, innovative or otherwise, has absorbed the construction techniques of the last ten years— consisting of components that are totally customizable, pre-engineered and prefabricated off site. And yet, single family residential developments generally emphasize guidelines concerning the character of the roof, while the shape has little impact on the interior. The roof form has largely been ignored in the arena of architectural speculation, because it is too loaded with issues of language and identity. Any innovation in the house type has to start from the top down.

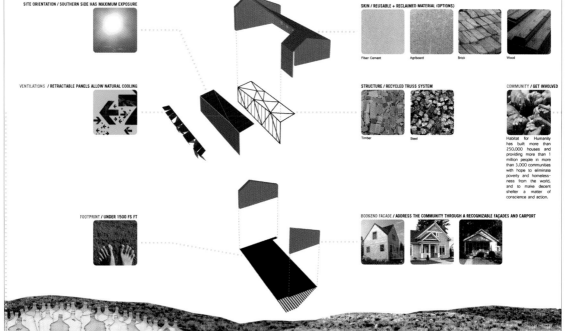

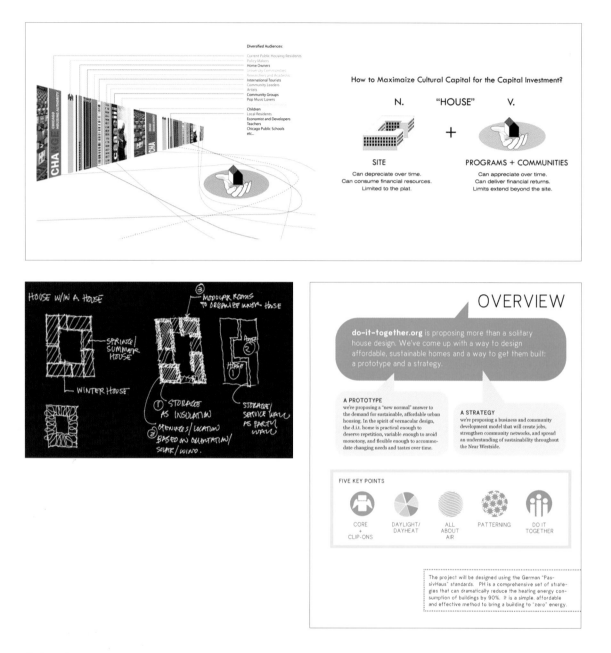

Clockwise from top:
Garofalo Architects, Chicago;
Studio THEM [Peter Lynch +
Gustavo Crembil], New York;
AWAKE Architecture, Knoxville, Tenn.

INDIVIDUAL HOMEOWNER PRIVATE/COMMERCIAL/RETAIL SPAC
NEW WALKABLE SERVICE

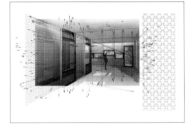

CORE+AIR

The "Core" is a modularly-built unit that incorporates efficient mechanical systems, the kitchen, and bathrooms. The rest of the structure acts as "Air." At the micro-scale, the Core is about designing for system efficiency in the individual home. At the macro-scale the Core has the potential to tie old and new homes into an environment-enhancing "greenbelt" infrastructure, creating community-wide energy savings, and other social benefits.

The Core accomplishes the following goals:

Sustainability
Affordability
Adaptive Reuse
Community Enhancement

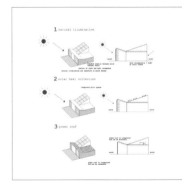

PAST
DENSE RESIDENTIAL FABRIC

PRESENT
DEMOLITION / REDEVELOPMENT

PROPOSED
REUSE / REPLACE

Clockwise from top:
Kuth/Ranieri Architects, San Francisco;
Workshop/apd, New York;
Fiedler Marciano Architecture,
New York; APTUM Architecture,
Berglatt, Switzerland

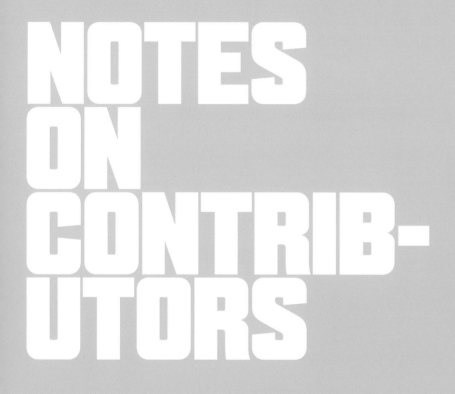

NOTES ON CONTRIB- UTORS

Andrew Bernheimer is a Brooklyn-based architect and principal of Bernheimer Architecture. Bernheimer was a founding partner of the award-winning firm Della Valle Bernheimer and teaches at Parsons The New School for Design. *Think/Make*, a monograph on the first decade of his practice at Della Valle Bernheimer, was published in 2009.

Stephen Cassell is principal and cofounder, with Adam Yarinsky, of Architecture Research Office (ARO). ARO is the 2011 winner of the Cooper-Hewitt National Design Award for Architecture, and last year the American Academy of Arts and Letters honored the firm with its Academy Award for Architecture. Selections of the firm's work appear in their monograph, *ARO: Architecture Research Office.* Cassell is a trustee of Van Alen Institute.

Rick Cook leads the award-winning design studio Cook+Fox Architects with long-time friend and partner Bob Fox. Over the past twenty-five years, Cook has pioneered sustainable design within the dense urban context, specifically forwarding the advancement of natural, biophilic design principles in New York City. In the summer of 2006, Cook and Fox joined green-building experts Bill Browning and Chris Garvin to form Terrapin Bright Green, a global strategic consulting firm that crafts high-performance environmental strategies.

Jared Della Valle has been a real estate professional and architect for more than fifteen years. He is president of Alloy Development LLC, a real estate development company he established in 2006 with partner Katherine McConvey. Della Valle was a founding partner of Della Valle Bernheimer (now known as Bernheimer Architecture), and is a member of the U.S. Green Building Council.

Susan Henderson is an architectural historian whose work has appeared in the *Journal of the Society of Architectural Historians*, *Journal of Architectural Education*, *Planning Perspectives*, *Design Issues*, and various other journals and edited volumes. She has written a book, *Building Culture: Ernst May and the New Frankfurt Initiative, 1925–1931*, forthcoming in 2012. She is a professor of architectural history at the School of Architecture at Syracuse University, where she also serves on the faculties of Society and Religion and the Middle Eastern Studies Program in the College of Arts and Sciences and is a member of the Center for European Studies in the Maxwell School.

Tim McDonald is an architect and a founding partner of Onion Flats in Philadelphia. He is as challenged and inspired by the multidisciplinary nature of architecture and building as he is by the art of communications with colleagues, clients, politicians, neighbors, contractors, and bankers. McDonald holds a B.Arch. from Pennsylvania State University and an M.Arch. in architectural history and theory from McGill University.

Mark Robbins is dean of the Syracuse University School of Architecture and the university's senior adviser for architecture and urban initiatives. Robbins served as director of design at the National Endowment for the Arts in Washington, DC, was curator of architecture at the Wexner Center for the Arts, and was an associate professor in the Knowlton School of Architecture at The Ohio State University. He received a fellowship in the visual arts from the Radcliffe Institute and a Rome Prize from the American Academy in Rome. He is the author of *Households*.

Michael Sorkin is principal of Michael Sorkin Studio, president of TERREFORM, and distinguished professor of architecture and director of the Graduate Program in Urban Design at the City College of New York. His most recent books are *Twenty Minutes in Manhattan* and *All Over the Map*.

Adam Yarinsky is principal and cofounder, with Stephen Cassell, of Architecture Research Office (ARO). Recent articles by Yarinsky have appeared in *a+u*, *306090*, *Dimensions*, and *Places*. He is also the coauthor of *On the Water: Palisade Bay*, which documents research performed as part of the 2007–9 AIA Latrobe Prize fellowship, an investigation into how rising sea levels will affect New York City.

Illustration Credits

14–17, 29: Mark Robbins ©2011

18, 19, 24, 26: Syracuse University, photographs by Steve Sartori ©2009

20–21, 24, 26, 29: UPSTATE: ©2011

36: Bild Design ©2008

37, 152 (center right): Konyk Architecture ©2008

38: Syracuse University School of Architecture ©2008

40, 151 (bottom left): Studio SUMO ©2008

41 (top): Atelier Mobius ©2008

41 (center), 150 (bottom left): Ackert Architecture/Dunne and Markis/Hood Design's ©2008

41 (bottom), 155 (center left): APTUM Architecture ©2008

42, 151 (top right): AGPS Architecture ©2008

43 (top), 154 (bottom left): AWAKE Architecture ©2008

43 (center): Workscape ©2008

43 (bottom), 155 (bottom left): Fiedler Marciano Architecture ©2008

44 (top): Burr and McCallum Architects ©2008

44 (center): Za Studio ©2008

44 (bottom), 155 (bottom right): Workshop/apd ©2008

45 (top): LOT-EK ©2008

45 (bottom): Cadwell Murphy ©2008

51, 58–66, 69, 76–86, 89, 97–104: Richard Barnes ©2011

52–57: Architecture Research Office and Della Valle Bernheimer ©2009

70, 72–75: Cook+Fox Architects ©2009

90, 92–96, 151 (bottom right): Onion Flats ©2009

109–15: Adjaye/Associates ©2008

117–27: Office dA and Studio Himma ©2008

129–35: do-it-together ©2008

139, 140, 142–46: Erdy McHenry Architecture and Stenson-Building+Furniture Design ©2008

150 (top): PLY Architecture ©2008

150 (center left): Griffin Enright Architects ©2008

150 (right): Eldorado, Inc. ©2008

151 (top left): Lang Architecture ©2008

152 (top left): Digsau Architecture ©2008

152 (top right): MOTOElastico [Simone Carena, Marco Bruno] ©2008

152 (bottom left): Archi-Tectonics ©2008

152 (bottom right): Goshow Architects©2008

153 (top left): GAutheir Architects ©2008

153 (top right): MOS Architects ©2008

153 (bottom): Studio Luz Architects ©2008

154 (top): Garofalo Architects ©2008

154 (bottom right): Studio THEM [Peter Lynch + Gustavo Crembil] ©2008

155 (top): Kuth/Ranieri Architects ©2008